BUDDHISM AND ETHNICITY

Social Organization of a Buddhist Temple in Kelantan

Mohamed Yusoff Ismail

Universiti Kebangsaan Malaysia

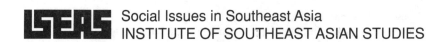

Social Issues in Southeast Asia
INSTITUTE OF SOUTHEAST ASIAN STUDIES

Cover

Monks chanting during dedication ceremony
of an archway, Bān Klāng, 1983

Published by
Institute of Southeast Asian Studies
Heng Mui Keng Terrace
Pasir Panjang Road
Singapore 0511

Cataloguing in Publication Data

Mohamed Yusoff Ismail.
  Buddhism and ethnicity : social organization of a Buddhist temple
in Kelantan.
  1. Theravāda Buddhism–Malaysia–Kelantan.
  2. Buddhism–Malaysia–Kelantan.
  3. Temples, Buddhist–Malaysia–Kelantan.
  4. Kelantan–Race relations.
  I. Title.
BQ569 M35M69   1993   sls92-31629

ISBN 981-3016-26-4 (hard cover)
ISBN 981-3016-27-2 (soft cover)

The responsibility for facts and opinions expressed in this publication rests exclusively with the author and his interpretations do not necessarily reflect the views or the policy of the Institute or its supporters.

Typeset by International Typesetters
Printed in Singapore by Singapore National Printers Ltd

BUDDHISM AND ETHNICITY

The **Institute of Southeast Asian Studies** was established as an auto-nomous organization in 1968. It is a regional research centre for scholars and other specialists concerned with modern Southeast Asia, particularly the many-faceted problems of stability and security, economic develop-ment, and political and social change.

The Institute is governed by a twenty-two-member Board of Trustees comprising nominees from the Singapore Government, the National University of Singapore, the various Chambers of Commerce, and profes-sional and civic organizations. A ten-man Executive Committee oversees day-to-day operations; it is chaired by the Director, the Institute's chief academic and administrative officer.

The **Social Issues in Southeast Asia (SISEA)** programme was established at the Institute in 1986. It addresses itself to the study of the nature and dynamics of ethnicity, religions, urbanism, and population change in Southeast Asia. These issues are examined with particular attention to the implications for, and relevance to, an understanding of problems of development and of societal conflict and co-operation. SISEA is guided by a Regional Advisory Board comprising senior scholars from the various Southeast Asian countries. At the Institute, SISEA comes under the overall charge of the Director, who is guided by an advisory committee com-prising senior regional scholars.

Dedicated to the memory of
Professor K.S. Sandhu
Director of ISEAS, 1972–1992

CONTENTS

LIST OF TABLES

LIST OF FIGURES

PREFACE

Buddhist religion of the Theravāda tradition, as embodied in the long-established temple institution and the monkhood, has been part of the rural scene in Kelantan for several hundred years. This study is about the Siamese and the organization of Theravāda Buddhism in a social and cultural context which is predominantly Malay and Islamic.

The relationship between Buddhism and Siamese ethnicity is a matter of primary interest here, at least in so far as it concerns ethnic relations in Kelantan. Even though Buddhism finds widespread adherence among various ethnic groups, it is among the Siamese that it flourishes and acquires a meaningful existence. In the context of Kelantan society, Theravāda Buddhism underwrites the basis of Siamese ethnic identity, while the continuity of Theravāda Buddhist tradition ensures such identity. In fact, the Siamese have been able to assert their identity *vis-à-vis* that of other groups in the larger society through their identification with Buddhism. This study will therefore examine the intricate process of ethnic identification and boundary maintenance as it evolves around temple organization and the management of its rituals.

While Siamese Buddhism as an institutionalized religion partly depends on Chinese financial and moral support, the Siamese conception and commitment to Buddhism differ in many ways from those of the Chinese. This cultural characteristic differentiates ethnically Siamese Buddhists from Chinese Buddhists. However, this observation is not to deny the fact that on numerous occasions Chinese do take great interest in temple rituals, not only by attending most of them but also by sponsoring some of them. Despite this, there are certain limitations with regard to their full involvement in the

Buddhist religion. For instance, while Chinese are known to have become monks, a great many do so for only a brief period, as a token of their adherence to the Theravāda tradition. In contrast, the Siamese are normally ordained for a much longer period. Whereas the Chinese are noted for their generosity in sponsoring temple cere- monies and in giving financial support to various temples, the corpus of specialized knowledge regarding Theravāda Buddhism is invested in the persons of village intellectuals and members of a religious élite who are almost exclusively Siamese.

There have been two major studies on the Siamese of Kelantan, namely, by Kershaw and Golomb. Kershaw's study of a coastal village of Semerak highlights the problems of integration of the Siamese into Malaysian social and political cultures (Kershaw 1969). The work by Golomb (1978) deals with the social and inter-ethnic behaviour of the Siamese in the context of a larger multi-ethnic society, particu- larly in their multi-faceted interaction with Malay villagers. The present study complements the works mentioned above. The greater part of the material presented here was collected during field-work done in Kelantan between April 1982 and October 1983.

This monograph is divided into several chapters. Chapter 1 briefly orients readers to the nature of ethnicity in Malaysian society and shows how the ideology of a plural society makes it necessary for people to stress their ethnicity by whatever means appropriate.

Chapter 2 analyses those aspects of Kelantan society which are directly relevant to the Siamese, particularly in a historical and cul- tural sense. The second part of the chapter introduces the reader to Bān Klāng, the pseudonymous village of study. Although about half of its population consists of Chinese, the village is characteristically Siamese because of its temple. Hence, in the absence of any other distinctive marker, the temple, as the main focus of social and reli- gious life, has been responsible for giving the village a cultural identity of its own, which contrasts markedly with surrounding Malay villages in the neighbourhood.

Chapter 3 provides an overview of the state's order of monks (*sangha*) and illustrates the dominance of the Siamese in the organ- ization of Theravāda Buddhist religion. The reality is that the Kelan- tanese Buddhist order of monks is essentially an extension of Thai- land's ecclesiastical organization.

Chapter 4 examines these roles more closely by looking at the social organization of the temple in Bān Klāng. Although members of the clergy are exclusively Siamese, the temple receives support from most households in the village regardless of whether they are Siamese or Chinese. Likewise, the temple also receives support from people outside the village who form part of its larger congregation, including Siamese and Chinese from other places. Despite the overwhelming support it receives from the Chinese, the temple as a religious and cultural institution remains characteristically Siamese in both form and content.

Chapters 5, 6, and 7 take up this point in greater detail; the participation of the Siamese in various temple functions serves to illustrate their level of adherence and commitment to Buddhism, which differs from that of the Chinese. The running of various temple affairs is handled by the Siamese and major decisions are made by a group of both religious and lay functionaries, who are almost exclusively Siamese. Chapter 8, the conclusion, reviews in broader terms the relationship of Buddhism to Siamese ethnic identity in Kelantan.

ACKNOWLEDGEMENTS

This book would not have materialized without the generous help of many people and institutions. I would like to thank the Institute of Southeast Asian Studies (ISEAS), Singapore, for providing me with a Research Fellowship under the Social Issues in Southeast Asia (SISEA) programme, funded by the Ford Foundation. My gratitude also goes to the Australian National University (ANU) for a post-graduate scholarship and a research grant to conduct field-work in Malaysia. Universiti Kebangsaan Malaysia provided me with study leave for the Ph.D. programme and permission to spend my sab-batical leave in Japan, where the final stage of the revision was done at the Graduate School of Area Studies, the University of Tsukuba, to which I also owe my gratitude.

Dr Douglas Miles gave me encouragement and advice during my study at the ANU; I have benefited tremendously from his sincere comments and meticulous supervision. I am also grateful to members of the Department of Prehistory and Anthropology of the ANU, especially to the late Professor Anthony Forge, Dr Geoffrey Benjamin, Dr Margo Lyon, and Dr Anthony Diller of the Faculty of Asian Studies, ANU.

I wish to acknowledge the kind assistance given by the Chief Monk of Kelantan, the late Phra Khrū Vicāranāyamūnī, and his deputy, Phra Khrū Opatdhammarat. The people of the village where my field-work was carried out were most co-operative and helpful, espe-cially the headman and his late father. The abbot of the village's temple, the monks, and other monastic residents gave me tremend-ous help and ensured that I was given the best possible treatment during my stay at the temple. Special thanks also go to the late *ācān wat* of the village, KhrūDaeng Phanthusān, my teacher and constant companion in the field. During the research period I visited many Siamese and Chinese villages and wherever I went I was received with warmth and sincerity by the people and monks, especially those of Aril, Bangsae, and the *nikhom* settlements in southern Thailand; to all of them I owe my gratitude.

I also wish to thank the Socio-Economic Research Unit of the Prime Minister's Department in Kuala Lumpur for permission to conduct research in Malaysia, and to the National Archives of Malaysia for access to historical documents.

My gratitude also goes to various people at ISEAS, especially the former Director, the late Professor K.S. Sandhu, the present Director, Professor Chan Heng Chee, Dr Sharon Siddique, Dr Ananda Rajah, and Mr Jalil Miswardi.

My wife, Zaharah, and my two children, Siti Zubaidah and Ahmad Mazlan, have always been my source of inspiration and emotional strength during the trying years of the research and writing of the manuscript. Clive S. Kessler and Shamsul A.B. gave me the courage to go on with the revisions; Clive read and kindly suggested various changes to the original draft; he is, however, not responsible for whatever flaws that remain, and the usual disclaimer applies.

TRANSCRIPTION
A Note on the Spelling of Thai Words

The transcription of standard Thai words in this book is based on Haas (1964). However, some modifications have been necessary. The four symbols used by Haas, namely, ɛ, ɔ, ə, and ŋ, have been replaced by combinations of letters found on the English typewriter keyboard. These are *ae, au, oe,* and *ng.* The first three are not diphthongs in the usual sense.

Haas' Symbols	Substitute Symbols			Examples		
ɛ	ae	แม่	*māe*	mɛɛ,	"mother"
ɔ	au	ขอ	*khāu*	khɔɔ,	"ask"
ə	oe	เดิน	*dōen*	dəən,	"walk"
ŋ	ng	งาน	*ngān*	ŋaan,	"work"

Long vowels are indicated by macrons such as *ā, ī,* and *ē.* The macrons are also used for vowels indicated by the substitute symbols above (*ae, au, oe*), such as *āu* in *māu* and *chalāung;* and *ōe* in *amphōe* and *batchōen.*

Final consonants จ, ด, ศ, ษ, and ส are represented by *t.* The Thai letter ก is represented by *k* instead of *g* if it occurs at the end of a syllable. No glottal stops are used.

Following Haas, *j* is pronounced like *y* as in the English "yell" if it is at the beginning of a syllable and similar to *i* if at the end of a diphthong.

The consonant *c* is not aspirated unless followed by an *h*. Likewise, all consonants preceding an *h* are aspirated. Hence, *ph* is aspirated while *p* is not.

Some words and place names have been spelt in styles other than that of Haas, such as *bhikkhu* (monk) (Haas: *phigsu*); *bhikkhuni* (female ascetic) (Haas: *phigsunii*); and *baht* (tical, monetary unit) (Haas: *baad*). I follow the former convention instead.

Thai is written without spaces between words. However, I have taken the liberty of putting spaces between words in certain terms so that they may be read more easily. Hence, *ton ngōen* is written with a space instead of *tonngōen*; *wan āsāahabūchā* instead of *wanāsālahabū-chā*; *thāut phā pā* instead of *thāutphāpā*; *phā ābnāmfon* instead of *phā-ābnāmfon*; and *Phra In* instead of *Phrain*.

I have made no attempt to reproduce the exact phonology of the Siamese dialect of Kelantan; hence, no tonal marks are used. Malay words are spelt according to the national spelling system currently in use, except where they occur in original quotations. Place names in Malaysia are spelt according to those used in the postcode guidebook issued by the Malaysian postal authority; but the spelling of place names which appear in direct quotations remain as they are found in the original text.

Chapter 1
Religion and Ethnicity

Ethnicity and Malaysian Society

The term "plural society" is often used to describe the particular form of society in which there are fundamental cleavages and discontinuities in social structure because of cultural, racial, or ethnic diversity. Pluralism, following the usage by Smith, is used in this study as a condition in which the members of a common society are internally distinguished by fundamental differences in their institutional practice (Smith 1971, p. 27). Malaysian society is pluralistic to the extent that it is never considered homogeneous because of the existence of various "ethnic" groups.

The classification of Malaysian population into ethnic categories is based on various criteria, the most common being geographical places of origin, dialect differences, and religious affiliation. For instance, the Malays as an ethnic group may consist of diverse groups of people that display cultural traits which are essentially Malay. Hence, within the broad definition of "Malay", Javanese, Sumatran, and other indigenous people from the Indonesian islands are placed into the same ethnic group. However, as an ethnic category, "Malay" is also defined, among other things, in terms of religious affiliation. The Malaysian Constitution, for instance, defines a "Malay" as one whose religious faith is Islam, who subscribes to the Malay custom, who speaks Malay, and who habitually lives a Malay way of life. Subsequently, the term *bumiputra* (literally, "children of the soil") is often used for a broader spectrum of ethnic categories which include other people who are not Muslim but whose cultural traits and practices are indigenous to the region. Hence, aboriginal groups of the Malay peninsula and indigenous groups in Sabah and Sarawak are also classified as *bumiputra.*

The Chinese, despite dialect variations among themselves and differences in geographical places of origin, are normally considered as a single ethnic category. This rather simplistic kind of categorization takes no account of the fact that the Chinese are not a homogeneous group. There have always been differences not only in terms of dialect, but also in their level of assimilation and acculturation to indigenous social and cultural traits. To illustrate this, there are Chinese who belong to the older wave of migration and who have been in this part of the Malay world for many centuries. Their cultural and social behaviour distinguishes them from those Chinese who belong to the new wave of immigration of less than one century.[1]

My data from Kelantan studies indicate that the majority of the Chinese who have been in Kelantan for many centuries normally have acquired some kind of religious affiliation with the Siamese, partly because of kinship relatedness, and partly because of the close social and cultural contact between the two groups. This characteristic has some bearing with regard to their cultural identification. This particular group of Chinese who appear to be full-fledged members of the local Buddhist congregation is distinguishable from the larger mainstream group of the Chinese population which typifies the west coast states of peninsular Malaysia. The former, known locally as Kelantan Chinese, are noted for their ease of assimilation into the local culture of the Malays. For this reason they may be identified as a group quite separate from the rest of the Chinese population of Malaysia. Their "front stage" behaviour is practically Malay in most respects.[2] Their main distinguishing characteristic, however, lies in the fact that they have their own system of religious belief, yet they are also known to be ardent supporters of Siamese Buddhism. These Chinese are generally known as *Cina kampung*, but more about this will be said later.

On the other hand, despite their apparent Malay-ness and their close association with Buddhist Siamese, Kelantan Chinese of the *Cina kampung* category could still theoretically identify themselves with the general Chinese community of Malaysia by other means. Since being Buddhist does not entail a loss of Chinese identity, a measure of fluidity tends to exist with regard to Chinese ethnic identification. The fluidity is in fact double-sided: on the one hand, a *Cina kampung* in Kelantan remains distinguishable from the rest of the larger Chinese community in Malaysia, and on the other, he may identify himself with the mainstream Chinese if he so wishes.

Ethnicity, Buddhism, and the Siamese

The Siamese is another ethnic category which makes up the ethnic composition of Kelantan. In this study the term "Siamese" refers to that particular group of people who openly claim themselves to be Siamese and are recognized as such by other ethnic groups. Such a claim is often supported by behaviour and mannerisms which are considered most appropriate for a Siamese, not only by the Siamese themselves but also by other ethnic groups as well. Foremost in the consideration of Siamese ethnic identity is the notion of a Siamese culture as embodied in the language, religion, historical sense, and tradition, and other attributes considered typically Siamese.

By virtue of their religion, the Siamese of Kelantan are differentiated from the Malays, who are predominantly Muslim. While religion, together with other objective criteria such as language, physical attributes, and other cultural characteristics may constitute an important aspect of Siamese ethnic identity, this alone is not adequate. It needs to be supported by the notion of "self-prescription" and "ascription by others" (Barth 1969, pp. 13, 14). For this reason any legitimate claim to an ethnic identity basically involves two things. First, a group or an individual must admit its sense of belonging to a particular ethnic group (Barth's "self-ascription"). Second, other ethnic groups within the same social system must recognize such a claim and honour it accordingly (Barth's "ascription by others"). These are basically two processes which cannot be separated from each other. Thus where only one of the two conditions obtains then there is room for uncertainty regarding one's ethnicity. Ethnicity is therefore a two-way process; first, one identifies oneself with an ethnic group by assuming the social and cultural behaviour associated with that particular group; at the same time such identification must be recognized by others, particularly by those already in the group one is identifying with and by those outside it. Once a claim is validated, other objective criteria including stereotypes and prejudices associated with a particular ethnic group set in, thereby helping to define further the ethnic category and strengthen its attributes.

Religion, as seen in Thailand, is also one of the defining characteristics of ethnicity. The predominance of Buddhism makes it the state religion of Thailand, and being a Thai (or Siamese) is equal to being a Buddhist. In Kelantan, although Buddhism does not occupy a similar position, Siamese ethnicity has always been closely identified with Buddhism. While many Chinese, Indians, and Sri Lankans in Kelantan also adhere to some form of Buddhism, the Siamese on the other hand emphasize the religious basis of their ethnicity by playing a dominant and crucial role in the social organization of the Buddhist religion. No other cultural attributes feature as strongly in the Siamese conception of ethnicity as Theravāda Buddhism. While Chinese and Indians may also practise other religions, such as Christianity and Hinduism, no Siamese in Kelantan are known to practise any religion other than Theravāda Buddhism.[3]

While Buddhism serves as the hallmark of Siamese ethnicity, the conscious need of the Siamese to emphasize their ethnicity *vis-à-vis* that of other groups is accomplished by their constant references not only to the Buddhist religion and its associated symbols (such as temple and monkhood) but also to things they and "others" perceive as culturally Siamese. To put it briefly, a spontaneously flourishing Buddhism ensures the existence and continuity of a Siamese ethnic identity in Kelantan and *vice versa*.[4] In this respect too, Golomb observes that generally there is a marked intensification of religious observation among the Siamese of Kelantan; he attributes this to the fact that in a plural society such as Malaysia, such an intensification is bound to happen for it helps to strengthen ethnic boundaries (Golomb 1978, p. 130). The Buddhist religion and its associated rituals and symbols, such as the temple (*wat*) and the Buddhist order of monks (*sangha*), therefore become crucial in so far as they concern Siamese ethnicity.

Apart from that, the notion of Siamese ethnicity may be seen in the expression of what Clifford Geertz has termed "primordial attachment" (1973, p. 259). Therefore, in the case of the Siamese, the concept encompasses various cultural elements which are considered typically Siamese, such as the Buddhist religion, the temple, the Siamese language, cultural preferences, and the incorporation of a "primordial attachment", which is exclusively Siamese.

The significance of Buddhism in underpinning Siamese ethnicity can only be understood if we consider the fact that in plural societies there is always a need to emphasize ethnicity, be it through religion, language, geographical place of origin, or any other means whatsoever. Malays, unlike the Chinese or the Siamese, are the only group whose ethnicity is constitutionally defined. Yet, the persistent need existing among other ethnic groups to emphasize their ethnicity has always been a salient feature of Malaysian society, to the extent that it virtually underlies nearly every aspect of social, political, and economic life. In fact, most Malaysians see themselves first as either Chinese, Malays, or Indians, and then only as "Malaysians". As a matter of prime consideration the ideology of multi-ethnic society makes it "virtually impossible to be ethnically 'neutral' by claiming no intervening ethnic status at all" (Nagata 1974, p. 33).

Buddhism, it is argued here, underlies Siamese ethnic identity but the Chinese too, especially rural-based Chinese, adhere to the same religion. While this appears quite problematic simply because by referring to religious criteria alone it is quite difficult to differentiate ethnically the Siamese from the Chinese, it is exactly from this very religious perspective that Chinese and Siamese Buddhists could be differentiated from each other. Although both are followers of Theravāda Buddhism, there is a fundamental difference between the two in terms of varying levels of commitment and adherence to the religion. While the Chinese support Buddhist temples generously and attend temple ceremonies with predictable regularity, it is the Siamese who play the crucial role in the custodianship of the ritual knowledge of the religion, hence its persistence and continuity. To use De Vos's terms, this is the "set of traditions" which the Siamese do not share with "others" (De Vos 1975, p. 9). There are, therefore, certain traditions cherished by the Siamese which form the basis of this ethnic differentiation. Thus while Chinese are also ordained, it is the Siamese who persist longest in the monkhood; while the Chinese bring material support to the temple, it is the Siamese who control the distribution of the gifts and their eventual use; whereas some Chinese are known as devout temple-goers, it is the Siamese who determine the precise running of temple events and ceremonies. These are religious behaviours which, when translated in terms of cultural characteristics, differentiate Siamese Buddhists from Chinese Buddhists. While adherence to a common religion tends to bring together Chinese and Siamese, it is the specialized role played by the Siamese in the management and the social organization of the religion which appears decisive in differentiating ethnically both ethnic groups from each other.

Siamese Buddhism in Kelantan

The fact that Kelantan is basically a Muslim state means that the local practice and organization of Buddhism must take place in a very specialized and adapted context, in a way which may differ from that of Thailand. The greatly emphasized social function of religion among the Kelantan Siamese becomes apparent when one considers the following factors:

First, Buddhist temples in Kelantan are symbolically important to the Siamese and, despite all odds against them, great efforts are made to maintain them in a fair degree of style and grandeur, although not necessarily similar in degree and magnitude to those in Thailand. While some of the more traditional functions of the temple may no longer exist, its basic functions in the social and religious spheres have never really diminished. The monastic institution may even have acquired some new meanings and roles which would probably not be of much significance had the temple been in Thailand. These new meanings and roles help to strengthen boundary markers, thereby further differentiating the Siamese from other ethnic groups.

Second, despite the fact that Siamese temples in Kelantan receive no direct financial assistance from the state or federal governments, most of them manage to enjoy a relatively comfortable existence. Temple funding comes partly from the local Siamese population, but a significant proportion also comes from the Chinese. In fact, one is most tempted to say that had it not been for the Chinese, many of the temples would suffer some kind of financial difficulties. Hence, the very survival of these temples depends very much on their ability to attract Chinese patronage.

Third, while it can be safely said that in Thailand social mobility in the larger society can be easily acquired if one has previously been ordained as a monk (because the elevated status so gained is highly regarded), the same may not be totally applicable in the case of Kelantan. Yet ordination activities in Kelantan temples are held quite regularly. This suggests that the monkhood still holds great import despite the fact that in Kelantan monastic experience does not usually contribute to social mobility within the larger society, to the degree that it does in Thailand. Ordination ceremonies are always regarded with seriousness and a deep sense of commitment by the Siamese; such activities not only promote their religious interests but also generate other benefits, including those economic and political.

The organization of the Buddhist religion in Kelantan must differ from that in Thailand if one takes into account the fact that Buddhism is accorded a different status in these two places. In Thailand Buddhism is the state religion, while in Kelantan and elsewhere in Malaysia it is not. This by itself contributes to certain complexities in the practice of Siamese Buddhism in Kelantan, that is, in an environment which is predominantly Malay and Islamic.

However, these complexities are self-resolving, for the Buddhism practised by the Siamese is not, as shown by Tambiah (1970), totally exclusive in nature, but is very accommodative indeed. For instance, there are certain practices which can be traced to existing religious beliefs, particularly those forms of animism which pre-dated Buddhism. As mentioned by Benjamin, a common theme running through most of the religious systems of Southeast Asia is that

> almost all the communities that claim allegiance to Islam, Christianity, or Buddhism also have recourse to animistic beliefs and practices. (Benjamin 1979, p. 24)

In Kelantan a similar phenomenon exists; to a limited extent the Siamese religion incorporates local elements of animism, those which typify Kelantanese Malays, those of local non-Malays, and those of Southeast Asia generally.

Even more complex is the fact that Siamese Buddhism in Kelantan also tolerates some elements of Chinese religion. For instance, a number of Siamese temples, especially those that have a considerable number of Chinese supporters, give some kind of recognition to one or two Chinese deities including the goddess Kuan Yin although she is definitely non-Siamese in origin. The Chinese who patronize Siamese temples seem to attach great importance to her, partly because she is highly relevant in terms of the belief system of Mahayana Buddhism. In some temples images of these dieties are often given a place although they are not necessarily erected at the most sacred location of the monastic compound. Apart from that, it is not uncommon for Siamese monks to get themselves invited to officiate at Chinese mortuary rites and other household ceremonies.

A political symbolism is also involved here: the formal Buddhist ecclesiastical organization of Kelantan recognizes the sultan of Kelantan, a Muslim, as its patron and as protector of the Buddhist religion in the state. The appointments of the chief monk and ecclesiastical district heads are endorsed by the sultan. This procedure illustrates the kind of accommodation the Siamese have made in order to give their ecclesiastical body some kind of political legitimacy, perhaps similar to that which exists in Thailand, where the king plays the same role. Thus in the absence of a Buddhist king, a Muslim ruler has been able to lend a "transcendental" dimension as the protector of the Buddhist religion in the state.[5]

This particular relationship between a Muslim ruler and a Buddhist community of monks (*sangha*) at first appears rather odd, but there is nothing exceptional in this. The role of the ruler is merely symbolic. Tambiah in his study of the religious system of northeast Thailand shows that

> the king was indeed the protector, defender and patron of the *sangha*, and at the apex of the society there is a fusion of politics and religion, spiritual and secular power, ... the king gave patronage to Buddhism: he built monasteries and temples, and endowed them with land. But he interfered little with ecclesiastical matters, and wherever monasteries were endowed with property they enjoyed autonomy in administering them, as well as judicial and fiscal exemptions and other immunities. (Tambiah 1970, p. 74)

In Kelantan, a similar conception of the state-*sangha* relationship in the political sense exists, modified only by the presence of a Muslim ruler. While a temple is exempt from paying taxes for the land on which it stands,[6] the ruler hardly interferes in the running of the day-to-day affairs of the monks and the *wat*, apart from giving his endorsement to the appointments of various ecclesiastical heads within the state *sangha*.

Apart from the special kind of relationship that exists between the state and the *sangha* there are two other important considerations which demand particular attention in the study of the Siamese of Kelantan. First, such an enquiry needs to consider the processes of change which most of West Malaysia's rural society has experienced to some degree in recent history. Second, the investigation must also focus on a phenomenon which is largely specific to the region where

I carried out my field-work: the rural population of Kelantan, apart from Malays and Siamese, also includes Chinese whose support of Buddhism appears to be highly relevant to the persistence of Siamese temples and by extension the institution of the monkhood.

The process of change, particularly the growth of the cash economy, has greatly affected many aspects of the social and cultural lives of rural areas. Many villages have been drawn into the larger market economy of the urban centres to the extent that economic and social relationships are now geared more towards these centres than towards their own neighbourhoods. Subsequently, traditional values that used to govern social relationship at the village level have either become redefined or replaced; the basis for a shared sense of village community has become eroded. In fact, to all intents and purposes, many of these villages have become a "dormitory" for people who work in urban centres, to which they return for rest at night, before the start of another working day.

The emerging pattern of the rural economy and the mismatch between it and the established pattern of social relationships within the village together mean that there is a need to redefine what really constitutes a village. While people still live within an environment that is very much village-like, their occupations may take them well outside the village boundaries. Although they return to the village regularly (daily for some, weekly or even monthly for others), they do not really belong to the village community except in a narrow and specific sense. When rural occupations become cash-oriented those institutions that help to bring villagers together, such as the communal sharing of labour, become bothersome if not irrelevant. In this sense the whole of the village community is no longer a single organic entity but rather divided into separate units, each confined to different households and family groups. Yet the pattern of residence in these Kelantan villages still conforms to rural style and does not indicate a great measure of urbanization. The concept of neighbourhood still endures although highly modified by urban values. In most Siamese villages, it is the institution of the temple that defines the social and physical limits of the village, even when everything else in rural society is breaking down and changing. Indeed, the more these changes occur, the more important the institution of the temple and the Buddhist religion become in defining the parameters of the village.

We now come to the second factor in this study: the "rural" Chinese of Kelantan. Although statistically, both "town" and "rural" Chinese are classified as a single ethnic group, basically there are fundamental cultural differences between the two. The majority of "urban" Chinese in Kelantan belong to the recent group of Chinese migrants that typifies the mainstream Chinese of the west coast states. While most urban-dwelling Chinese are descendants of late nineteenth and early twentieth century immigrants, most of the rural-based Chinese are descendants of those who arrived much earlier, perhaps as early as the fifteenth century. Chinese immigrants of earlier periods, normally well received by the local Malays, settled in rural areas where they are known as "rural Chinese" (*Cina kampung*), whose social and cultural values have been greatly influenced by the Malays.[7] Even today this earlier group of Chinese consider themselves more *Malayanized* than the mainstream Chinese, in many ways similar to the *baba* group of Melaka, Pulau Pinang, and Singapore.[8]

Rural-dwelling Chinese, because of their long association with the local Malays, are more oriented towards the local culture than the group of Chinese that arrived more recently. In Melaka the group of "old" Chinese known as *baba* trace their ancestry to the fifteenth century immigrants. In Indonesia the "old" group of Chinese, who have adopted the indigenous culture while still remaining Chinese at the same time, are known as *peranakan*. As a contrast the second group, that is, the "new" Chinese, are called *totok*.

In Kelantan the term *peranakan* is seldom used to describe the Chinese of ancient immigration.[9] Nevertheless, Kelantan Malays generally make quite a clear distinction between the two groups of Chinese. The "older" group of Chinese are known by various names, but all the terms used point to one thing, namely, the level of assimilation this particular group has gone through. Hence, the following terms are used for the "old" Chinese: *Cina kampung* (village Chinese), *Cina Kelantan* (Kelantan Chinese), *Cina tempatan* (local Chinese), and *Cina sini* (Chinese "of here"). Some Kelantan Malays even refer to the earlier group of Chinese, rather affectionately, as *orang Cina kita* (our Chinese). The recently arrived Chinese, that is, the "new" group, are known in Kelantan either as *Cina luar* (outsider Chinese) or *Cina benua* (literally, Chinese of the Chinese "continent").[10] The Siamese also make a clear distinction between the "old" Chinese, whom they call *cīn bok*, and the "new" Chinese, whom they refer to as *cīn myang* (Golomb 1978, p. 82).

The rural Chinese are noted for their close association with the Malays, and their adaptability to and superb knowledge of Malay culture. It is often the case that their children are educated at Malay schools, some even taking and excelling in Islamic religious studies. Most of their "front stage" behaviour is overtly and deliberately Malay to the extent of speaking Malay even at home among themselves. Over the course of time a number of these earlier migrant Chinese have converted to Islam with their subsequent decendants "becoming Malays".[11]

In this study I have used the term "Kelantan Chinese" interchangeably with "rural Chinese" (*Cina kampung*) for want of a better term. The word "rural" here does not necessarily mean that all the earlier migrant Chinese are presently rural dwellers, but rather that they have adapted to rural Malay culture to the point of acquiring many Malay folk attributes. The urban Chinese in contrast are not necessarily Malay in behaviour and mannerisms. Chinese of earlier migration who display overtly Malay folk behaviour may also live in town areas and engage in trades and the professions, but their mannerisms and cultural behaviour make them easily distinguishable from the rest of the Chinese population in the town. Apart from this, the rural Chinese of Kelantan have special privileges with regard to land ownership. Like the Siamese they are among the few non-Malay groups with legal titles to ownership of lands in Malay Reservation areas.[12] Because of this many do have "ancestral homes" in rural villages of Kelantan to which they return regularly, typically during Chinese festive occasions. Perhaps this is another criterion that sets them apart from the mainstream Chinese.

Although the majority of the "rural" Chinese have adopted much of the local Malay culture they have not become Muslims. They have their own system of worship as typified by belief in the guardian gods of the village and patron deities of the house. Apart from the worship of their respective village deities, the rural Chinese also patronize Siamese temples and take part in Buddhist rites and ceremonies. It is in this sense that Siamese Buddhism has also become the basis of identity for the rural Chinese *vis-à-vis* the larger, mainstream Chinese group. Through their participation in the rituals they become members of the same religious and social community as the Siamese.

Their close association with the Siamese is perhaps attributable to their settlements being located quite close to, and often constituting part of Siamese villages, and to the kin relationships deriving from intermarriage between the two groups during the early period of Chinese migration to the region. Although intermarriage between the Siamese and the rural Chinese is not as common as it used to be, these kinship ties are widely acknowledged today even if neither group can trace their genealogy with precision. However, this special relationship between the Siamese and the rural Chinese is not without some negative effect on the latter. Other Chinese groups, especially those of the west coast and the urban-based, tend to consider the rural Chinese culturally less "Chinese" because of their close association with the Siamese and because of the usage among themselves of a peculiar version of Hokkien dialect. Consequently, other groups of Chinese often refer to the rural Chinese as "Hokkien-Siam", a term which the latter find very condescending if not offensive.[13] The rural Chinese feel that despite their Chinese origin, they are being looked down upon by the Chinese that arrived more recently. The other cultural characteristic of the rural Chinese, that of being acculturated towards the Malays, is also one of the factors which differentiate the rural Chinese from other groups of Chinese.

However, the issue of the rural Chinese identifying themselves with the Siamese religious tradition is very important here. Although theoretically the rural Chinese have the option of identifying themselves with the larger Malaysian Chinese community they have chosen not to do so, at least not to a large extent for now. In fact, there are real barriers to their doing so. For a start the rural Chinese are different from the mainstream Chinese not only linguistically, but also culturally. They are more established in the rural areas, more enculturated into the norms and values of the local population and feel more at ease among the rural folk. Futhermore, the rural Chinese, with few exceptions, are socially and economically more tied to land, unlike the majority of the mainstream Chinese of Kelantan who are involved in urban types of occupations such as trading, retailing, business, and the professions.

Given the rural nature of their orientation, Chinese of the ancient immigration are more inclined to identify themselves with the Siamese rather than with the mainstream Chinese. Their identification with the Siamese is the natural choice, and Kershaw gives two reasons for this. First, because of the hostility the Malays had towards the earlier Chinese immigrants, especially regarding intermarriage with them, previous generations of the rural Chinese tended to seek Siamese women as marriage partners. Second, they chose to be involved with the Siamese because of their familiarity with Buddhism, even if not of the Theravāda kind. For these reasons, it has been quite usual for many of the earlier migrant Chinese to establish their residence close to or in Siamese villages (Tan 1982, p. 34; Kershaw 1973, p. 5, n. 12). Because of the close relationship, genealogically and socially, between the rural Chinese and the Siamese, the former are often referred to by other Chinese groups as Hokkien-Siam or *cīn thaj*, another trait which sets apart the rural Kelantan Chinese from the mainstream Chinese.

The long-established kinship ties between the rural Chinese and the Siamese are constantly recognized and validated, most obviously during temple functions. A significant proportion of the rural Chinese who attend these functions acknowledge their kinship relations with the Siamese, no matter how remote they have now become. In the light of this consideration a Buddhist temple, therefore, becomes the focal point and a social magnet which brings together the Siamese and the Chinese of Kelantan under a common interest; and participation in temple ceremonies ritualizes this special alliance.

On the whole it can be stipulated that, because of the various factors mentioned above, the Siamese and Chinese living far afield are drawn together to the same temple during festive and religious occasions. Monetary and moral support derived from the "outside" economy enable Siamese Buddhist temples to organize regularly various religious and social undertakings through the intermediary of Theravāda monks and Siamese religious élites. Thus, despite ethnic differentiation between Chinese Buddhists and Siamese Buddhists, existing economic and social linkages bind the Siamese temples with the larger world beyond the threshold of the village. The intricacies in this kind of relationship, frequently acted out within the boundary of the temple ground, result in the reproduction of various Siamese religious forms and cultural expressions, apparently all contributing towards the enhancement and perpetuation of Siamese ethnic identity.

The Usage of the Term "Siamese"

In this study I use the term "Siamese" in preference to "Thai", although others (for example, Kershaw, Golomb, Winzeler, and Tan)
have used the latter term. As I have argued elsewhere, the term
"Thai" is necessarily of recent import in Kelantan, just as it is in
Thailand itself (Ismail 1977, 1980*a*, 1982).[14] As an ethnic group they
have always been known as *orang Siam* not only in Kelantan but also
elsewhere in the northern Malay states. Although among themselves,
the Siamese may refer to one another as *khon thaj*, the term "Thai"
appears to have gained limited currency in the everyday parlance of
other ethnic groups, who prefer to use *orang Siam* instead. Nevertheless, the term "Thai" has recently become quite fashionable,
especially among the few who have received formal schooling in
Thailand or who have spent some time as monks there, but its actual
usage in the context of inter-ethnic communication in Kelantan is
somehow limited. For this reason I prefer to use the English term
"Siamese" for the ethnic group known either as *khon thaj* or *orang
Siam.*

Thailand is frequently referred to as *Negeri Siam* by most Kelantanese. Hence, the kingdom is commonly known among Malays as
Balik Siam or *Balik Barat.*[15] The term *orang Siam* is the Malay word for
the Siamese people. Whenever there is a need to differentiate the
Siamese of Kelantan from those of Thailand, then *orang Siam sini* is
used for the former in contrast to *orang Siam Bangkok* or *orang Siam
barat* for the latter. Most interesting, however, is the fact that among
themselves the Siamese persistently use the term *"khāek"* to refer to
the Malays, although they refrain from using it when Malays known
to understand the Siamese language are within earshot. In Thailand
khāek in its formal sense means "guest" but it now carries a derog-
atory connotation especially with respect to the Malays of southern
Thailand (Burr 1972, p. 185).

NOTES

1. For a discussion of this, see Wang (1978).
2. For the origin and usage of this term, see Raybeck (1980, pp. 252, 254).
3. I have mentioned the Theravāda school because in Kelantan there are

no full-fledged Mahayana Buddhist temples as such. The latter temples may be found in other parts of Malaysia and Singapore, especially in association with Chinese temples, but none, staffed by full-time monks, are known to exist in Kelantan. In general the Chinese identify with either school of Buddhism. The Siamese of Kelantan identify exclusively with the Theravāda tradition.

4. A similar observation is also made by Kershaw in his study of the Siamese of Semarak, in the district of Pasir Puteh (1969, p. 166).

5. I have briefly mentioned this elsewhere (Ismail 1977, pp. 76, 77; 1982, p. 255).

6. Land on which a temple stands is considered similar to *wakaf* land, that is, land specifically endowed for public use, for example, for the purpose of erecting a mosque or for a public cemetery.

7. An exception to this is the Chinese settlement of Pulai in Ulu Kelantan, where the immigrants, mainly Hakka-speakers, remained character- istically Chinese, experiencing very little assimilation into the indi- genous culture. Because of the imbalance in the sex ratio, some of the men married aboriginal (*Orang Asli*) and Siamese women, but this did not help to assimilate them like other "rural Chinese". For more details on the Chinese settlement of Pulai, see Middlebrook (1933, pp. 151– 56); for a recent work on the same settlement, see Carstens (1980, pp. 50–67); see also Downs (1967).

8. For a more detailed discussion of earlier Chinese settlements in Kelantan, see Middlebrook (1933), Carstens (1980), and Cushman and Milner (1979). On *baba* Chinese, see, for instance, Tan (1979). For accounts of "rural" Chinese or the earlier group of Chinese immigrants, see Winzeler (1974, 1981), Kershaw (1981), and Tan (1982). That earlier Chinese migrants met little opposition from the Malay peasantry could have been due to the fact that the former must have arrived at a time when good agricultural lands were still abundant. Moreover, residence patterns seem to indicate that the Chinese did not compete with the Malays for land, because the former chose to occupy less fertile land, usually quite close to rivers, while the latter preferred, for their padi-cultivation, land away from the river banks (Winzeler 1981, p. 7).

9. Only researchers tend to use *peranakan* for want of a better term. Tan (1982, p. 31), for instance, uses a similar term but not without any cautionary remarks when describing the acculturated Kelantan or "rural" Chinese, for there is no exact term applicable to their case.

10. Apparently, in the conception of traditional Kelantanese view, China is referred to as a continent (*benua*). In classical Malay literature and

oral traditions this is also the usual term used. Thus *benua China* means the "Chinese kingdom" (literally, the Chinese "continent"). "Urban" Chinese are also derogatorily referred to as *Cina tok pek* (Tan 1982, pp. 29–30, n. 8).

11. The most commonly used local term for this is *masuk Melayu*. It has been a widespread practice for Chinese converts to be given the honorary title of "Che" as part of their Muslim names. Although the term "Che" in standard Malay (now spelt "Cik") is an abbreviation of "Inche" and equivalent to the English "Mr", in Kelantan it often becomes an integral part of personal names. The title being hereditary, many people who bear it are believed to be descendants of converts from other ethnic groups, mainly Chinese and Indians.

12. The same privileges are also enjoyed by the Siamese in other northern states of Malaysia, in particular Kedah and Perlis (Mokhzani 1973, p. 10).

13. The Kelantan version of the Hokkien dialect has absorbed many Malay and Siamese terms to the extent that it is understood with difficulty outside the rural Chinese circle. Chinese from other parts of the country, particularly from the west coast states, even if they are Hokkien speakers, may have difficulty understanding the Kelantan version of the dialect.

14. On the history of the usage of the term "Thai" see, for instance, Surin (1982). The term "Thailand" (with emphasis on "Thai") was first introduced in June 1939 during the time of Pibul Songkhran to replace the more neutral term "Siam" (ibid., p. 89). It was during this period that efforts intensified to create a sense of Thai nationalism in the face of new challenges from the rapid process of modernization. The extent to which such efforts have influenced the ethnic perception of the Siamese of Malaysia is not very clear, but the term "Siamese" continues to enjoy wide usage in Kelantan and other northern states.

15. *Orang barat* conveys the popular meaning of someone from Thailand or further north of the Malay peninsula. In Kelantanese Malay dialect, *barat* does not mean "west" as in standard Malay, but rather north and northeasterly; see Brown (1956, p. 166) and Pepys (1916, p. 306).

Chapter 2
The Research Area and the Village of Study

The Historical Link between Kelantan and Siam

Prior to the twentieth century local politics in the northern Malay states used to be dominated by a sovereign power emanating from the kingdom of Siam. The support of the Siamese king and his princely representatives was crucial to the outcome not only of wars between Malay rulers and district chiefs but also of feuds for succession to Malay thrones.

The role of Siam in the affairs of the Malay states has been covered by a number of scholars.[1] However, the point that is relevant to the present study is that the mere political presence of Siam as a superpower that the Malay states had to acknowledge was highly conducive to the movement of Siamese settlers southwards into Kelantan river plain. Hence, the original Siamese settlers seemed to have been able to enjoy some kind of advantage and freedom resulting from the *présence siamoise* at the higher level of political relation between Kelantan and Siam. Any expression of open hostility or resistance to the south-bound migrating Siamese peasants was therefore most unlikely, especially by the local chiefs, for fear that opposition raised against Siamese settlements in Kelantan could possibly strain relationship between local Malay rulers and their Siamese overlord. The former could ill-afford such tension since they lived under constant surveillance by Siam.[2] Nor are there recorded cases of Malay opposition against the setting up of settlements by the Siamese in Kelantan.

It seems that the establishment of peasant settlements in Kelantan was not in any sense an outcome of a "colonial" policy on the part of the Siamese kingdom. Whatever political interest the Siamese kingdom had in the Malay states was not for the sake of establishing Siamese outposts, but to gain military and material support in its campaign against its Burmese neighbour and the British. Certainly no Siamese villages are known to have been established by royal decree from Bangkok (Kershaw 1973, p. 4). The earlier history of Kelantan prior to the beginning of the present century supports the general picture that Siam had influence, although of varying nature and degree, in the internal affairs of Malay states.[3] Historically, Kelantan is related to Thailand through its close ties with other Malay states in the southern part of present-day Thailand, particularly Patani (Wyatt 1974, pp. 2–3).

Vella also asserts that there had been variations in the suzerain-vassal relationship:

> The nearer vassals were subjected to greater control than the ones farther from the Siamese territory, and all vassals were closely bound to Bangkok during the period when the Bangkok government was strong. (Vella 1957, p. 61)

Thus the real power of Siam over the affairs of the Malay states during the late nineteenth century depended on its ability to enforce its suzerainty over these states. A powerful ruler at the centre could exert more influence and control over the peripheral Malay states, but if this power were to wane "so too did submission on the part of the dependency" (Sharom Ahmat 1971, p. 97).

Kelantan was one of the vassal states at the outer fringes and as such had managed to escape the stringent political control of the Siamese. Yet the Siamese influence still manifested itself at the most crucial moments, such as during the feuds for succession to the throne. Apart from that, Kelantan had to send to Bangkok the tri-ennial tribute of gold in the form of a ceremonial tree (Malay: *bunga mas*).[4] In addition, Malay rulers and principal officers of Malay sultanates were given titles and insignia of office by the Siamese king (Vella 1957, p. 60).

Due to the geographical proximity of Siam and Kelantan, it is not surprising that some aspects of Kelantanese culture have been considerably influenced by the Siamese. For instance, the local Malay dialect of Kelantan is interspersed with many Siamese terms,[5] and Kelantanese Malay magic and ritual include components that are of Siamese origin. The Malays acknowledge such influence by referring to the shadow-puppetry in their community as *wayang Siam*. Whether Malay or Siamese, a puppeteer precedes a performance with an almost identical ritual and draws on the same repertoire of stories. Buddhist ritual objects, such as the monks' bowl and sacralized water, *nāmmon*, often become a source of magic and fear for the Malays.

It is with this kind of historical backdrop that the Siamese peasants have established themselves in Kelantan. No researchers have been able to determine exactly when the Siamese first came to Kelantan. But a safe estimate is that many of these villages were established more than one hundred years ago or at least around the late nineteenth and early twentieth centuries. Some villages are known to have been in existence for more than 150 years. There are various oral traditions relating to Siamese ancestors who came to Kelantan as first pioneers. For instance, a Siamese settlement in Semerak attributes its origin to a group of people sent "somewhere from Bangkok" or Sukothai in search of a king's lost white elephant. Since they were unsuccessful in finding the animal they decided to settle down locally rather than return home and risk the death penalty for their failure (Kershaw 1969, p. 81). That incident was supposed to have taken place at a time beyond anyone's living memory.

A Siamese village in Kelantan studied by Golomb has an oral tradition that its original settlers were actually a group of adventurous young people known as the *naklēng*,[6] who roamed the countryside in search of game and good hunting grounds. They were also accomplished *manōrā*[7] players who performed at various places that they passed by. It was further said that their performance had so impressed a local Malay chief that they were invited to settle down in a village under the chief's jurisdiction. The Siamese village which I studied earlier, Aril, echoes similar lines in its oral history; it was originally a settlement the Malays abandoned. Eventually reverting itself to jungle, it became infested with a thriving colony of wild pigs that caused considerable damage to crops grown in neighbouring Malay villages. Consequently a *naklēng* group that passed through the district was offered by the local chief to reopen the village, thus helping to stamp out the wild pigs, and at the same time increasing the population of the area.

The Population of Kelantan:
The Ethnic Composition

More than 90 per cent of Kelantan's population in 1980 is Malay. The Chinese form the second largest ethnic group, followed by the Siamese, who slightly outnumber the Indians (Table 2.1). Although the Siamese were originally immigrants, they nevertheless differ in many respects from other non-indigenous ethnic groups of Malaysia. In the first place, the Siamese are not of recent origin and were established in the state before the massive influx of the Chinese and the Indians during the early part of this century. Secondly, in comparison with other ethnic groups, the Siamese are the least urbanized, with more than 90 per cent of them living in rural areas. The Chinese are highly urbanized by comparison with other ethnic groups in Kelantan, and this pattern follows the trend throughout the country; more than half of the Chinese reside in larger towns.[8] The Hokkien speakers, who number 26,782, are the largest Chinese dialect group in Kelantan. They comprised more than 59 per cent of the state's Chinese population in 1980. Of the Hokkien speakers, 47 per cent or 12,661 live in rural areas. This number of rural-based Hokkien group is bigger than the combined total of rural dwellers of other Chinese dialect groups (Table 2.2). The majority of rural Chinese who support the Siamese temples comes from the Hokkien dialect group.

TABLE 2.1
Kelantan: Population by Ethnicity and Stratum, 1980

Ethnicity	Urban	Rural	Total	% of Total State Population
Malay	210,091 (26.3%)	588,670 (73.7%)	798,761	93.1
Chinese	26,010 (57.8%)	18,957 (42.2%)	44,967	5.2
Siamese	737 (9.8%)	6,820 (90.2%)	7,557	0.9
Indian	2,857 (46.7%)	3,265 (53.3%)	6,122	0.7
Others	523 (66.7%)	261 (33.3%)	784	0.1
Total	240,218	617,973	858,191	100.0

SOURCE: Government of Malaysia, *1980 Population and Housing Census of Malaysia* (1983).

TABLE 2.2

Kelantan: Chinese Population by Dialect Group, 1980

Dialect	Urban	Rural	Total	% of Dialect Group over Total Number of Chinese
Hokkien	14,121 (52.7%)	12,661 (47.3%)	26,782	59.6
Cantonese	3,897 (62.8%)	2,309 (37.2%)	6,206	13.8
Khek (Hakka)	2,986 (59.3%)	2,047 (40.7%)	5,033	11.2
Teochew	1,544 (81.8%)	344 (18.2%)	1,888	4.2
Hainanese	2,264 (79.9%)	569 (20.1%)	2,833	6.3
Kwongsai	130 (18.9%)	557 (81.1%)	687	1.5
Hokchiu	150 (67.9%)	71 (32.1%)	221	0.5
Hokchia	20 (54.1%)	17 (45.9%)	37	0.1
Henghua	338 (85.4%)	58 (14.6%)	396	0.9
Other dialects	560 (63.3%)	324 (36.7%)	884	1.9
Total	26,010 (57.8%)	18,957 (42.2%)	44,967	100.0

SOURCE: Government of Malaysia, *1980 Population and Housing Census of Malaysia* (1983).

The Village of Bān Klāng

I name the village of study Bān Klāng, which is a pseudonym. During my field-work in 1982 and 1983 there were altogether 126 households in the settlement, with a total population of 528 people in October 1983. This figure is but a rough estimate because of the "floating" nature of the population. For instance, there are five vacant houses whose owners, then living outside the village, return only occasionally. Many people who belong to a particular household may not have been staying in Bān Klāng at the time the census was conducted, yet they are still counted as members of the household. Being "absentee" members, these people normally stay at their workplaces during weekdays but return to the village at regular intervals, particularly during the weekends and major temple festivals, or whenever family matters needed to be attended to personally. They nevertheless constitute an integral part of the household because of their contribution towards its total income. Since this particular group of people display no definite pattern of residence, they may be termed "floating". Typical of these are younger people who move back and forth as they please between their workplaces and their parents' house in the village.

In contrast with other Siamese villages, Bān Klāng has no legend regarding its establishment.[9] The original settlers are believed to have come from another village located further inland, which is now populated by Malays. It is not clear why they moved from Tok Mekong to Bān Klāng, but one theory is that the availability of large tracts of good, low-lying land suitable for rice-farming around the village must have prompted the move. The people of Bān Klāng do not remember exactly when their ancestors first came to settle on the present site, but some of the older residents still recall their ancestors telling them that during those days there were few Malay villages in the area. There was, therefore, little or no competition for land when the Siamese first established themselves in Bān Klāng.

Bān Klāng consists of several sectors, each consisting of a cluster of houses. The central sector of the village is located at the crossroads where a number of sundry shops and a government clinic are located (Map 2.1). The village's temple, however, is located not in the central sector, but rather in an exclusive sector away from residential areas. With regard to sub-district administration, Bān Klāng comes under the jurisdiction of a government-appointed headman, who is ethnically Chinese.

While most of the sectors of Bān Klāng have a mixed population of Siamese and Chinese households, there is one sector which is almost exclusively Chinese. This particular sector consists of twenty-five households, all of which are Chinese (that is, heads of households and spouses, with the exception of one, whose wife is Siamese). Chinese are also found in other sectors but they are heavily out-numbered by the Siamese. Because of its total Chinese population the sector mentioned could be easily mistaken for another village quite apart from Bān Klāng. But this sector is essentially an integral part of Bān Klāng's social and religious community, not only because it shares the same government-appointed headman, but also because most of its households support the village's temple as do the rest of the population. For example, every household in the Chinese sector observes its turn to send food to the temple's resident monks in accordance with a roster system in which almost all Bān Klāng households are involved.[10] If we consider participation in temple rituals as indicative of membership of the community, then the Chinese house-

MAP 2.1
Bān Klāng

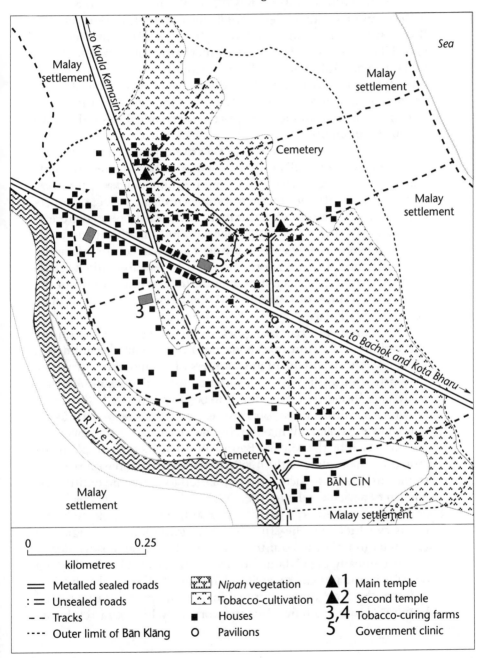

Sea

Malay settlement

to Kuala Kemasin

Malay settlement

Cemetery

Malay settlement

Malay settlement

to Bachok and Kota Bharu →

River

Cemetery

BĀN CĪN

Malay settlement

Malay settlement

| 0 | 0.25 |
| kilometres |

— Metalled sealed roads
∶= Unsealed roads
- - Tracks
---- Outer limit of Bān Klāng

▦ *Nipah* vegetation
▦ Tobacco-cultivation
■ Houses
O Pavilions

▲1 Main temple
▲2 Second temple
3,4 Tobacco-curing farms
5 Government clinic

holds in this sector are certainly part of that collectivity.

Until recently, Bān Klāng was one of the most isolated Siamese settlements in Kelantan. Before 1980, the usual connection between Bān Klāng and the state capital, Kota Bharu, was by a surfaced road of 45 kilometres long. There was an alternative route to Kota Bharu by a dirt road. Although the distance was much shorter, one had to use a ferry to cross a river which flows west of Bān Klāng. When a bridge was built and the dirt road surfaced with asphalt in 1980, the driving distance from Bān Klāng to the state capital was reduced to a mere 15 kilometres.

An important feature of Bān Klāng's present economy is that it is no longer based on padi-growing, as it used to be some ten to twenty years ago. Tobacco is now grown commercially, almost to the complete exclusion of other crops. Another significant aspect of its economy is that a considerable number of Bān Klāng people are employed outside the village itself, especially in Kota Bharu and other smaller towns in Kelantan. Employment in urban centres including Kuala Lumpur and Singapore also contributes substantially to the income of some Bān Klāng households. Indeed most youths of the village have found jobs outside and many reside temporarily at or near their workplaces.

The economy of Bān Klāng before the 1960s was based on the cultivation of rice and market-gardening. The area around Bān Klāng is low-lying and the pioneer settlers who established the village were attracted to it by the abundance of land suitable for rice-cultivation. Rice-growing continued to be of importance to the village until the early 1960s when tobacco was gradually introduced into the neighbouring villages. While the commercial growing of tobacco was first practised by the Malays, Bān Klāng villagers did not plant the crop until the middle of the 1960s, initially in rotation with rice, but by the early 1970s tobacco-growing started to dominate entirely the pattern of agricultural land use.

Commercial tobacco-growing in Bān Klāng is part of the larger industry which supplies flue-cured Virginia leaves to cigarette manufacturers in the country. The industry was first started by a private company, the Malayan Tobacco Company (MTC) in 1959 but over the years, and after a crisis which nearly led to a collapse of the industry, the government stepped in, and the previous role played by the MTC was taken over by a statutory body, Lembaga Tembakau

Negara (National Tobacco Board [NTB]), formed in August 1973, whose main responsibility includes supervision, research, and overall control of the industry.[11] The NTB issues licences to companies and co-operatives involved in the tobacco-curing business. Growers are required to register themselves with curers of their choice, to whom they are contracted to sell their harvest. Curers in return also act as agents for the NTB and are responsible not only for giving technical advice and supervision to registered growers but also for extending the credit facilities and fertilizer subsidies provided by the NTB. The visible effect of tobacco-growing as a cash crop is that the agricultural cycle in the village is now determined by curers who make most of the major decisions regarding the cultivation of the crop. All agricultural work is, therefore, geared towards the enterprise that the curers control.

Significantly, tobacco-growing has been carried out to the exclusion of all other crops. The reason for this is not exactly clear, for tobacco occupies the land for only less than six months of the year, leaving the land free for other crops for the rest of the year. Yet no other crop is grown, not even watermelon, which is suited to the type of soil around the village. Another crop that could be grown outside the tobacco season is rice, which was the traditional crop cultivated before the shift to tobacco. However, compared with tobacco, rice gives a poorer economic return for the same amount of labour and capital investment. Perhaps the incentive to grow rice is offset by the easy availability of cheaper and better-quality smuggled Thai rice. Another likely reason for this lack of interest in rice cultivation is that workers of many households in Bān Klāng find that income from off-season employment outside the village is more lucrative than that derived from growing rice in the village.

The tobacco-growing season, covering a period of nearly five months, starts from early December, when seed beds are prepared, and ends about April when the last leaves are harvested. In Bān Klāng there is only one growing season per year although other places practise double-cropping. As the growing season is short there is a lull of about six months in village agricultural activity during which villagers take on outside jobs to supplement household income.

As tobacco-cultivation is labour-intensive, it is during the growing season that additional labour is required to help out in the field. This extra labour comes from two main sources. First, people who are

originally from Bān Klāng but are now temporarily employed outside
the village return to give assistance, resuming their former jobs at the
conclusion of the season. Second, some households that plant no
tobacco assist others in the field. Elderly women and men, otherwise
unemployed during other times of the year, often work on tobacco
patches belonging to friends and relatives.[12]

Harvested leaves are sold to the two tobacco-processing companies in Bān Klāng, each of which operates a curing station. Both
companies are owned by groups of Bān Klāng residents; their shareholders, with the exception of one Siamese male, are Chinese of the
Cina kampung type. The curing stations also provide employment,
mainly from March to August, to many women of Bān Klāng and
neighbouring Malay villages. Each station employs between fifty and
eighty people to sort and grade harvested leaves. After August only
five to eight Malay men continue to work the kilns.

Nearly all households derive some income from growing or
processing tobacco. I have no figures of the exact cash returns each
household in the village derives from the sale of its tobacco harvest.
Moreover, most households do not keep accurate accounts in terms
of capital outlay, expenses, and income associated with tobacco-
growing. Because of the credit advance given by the NTB through
the curers, growers appear to be receiving less money than they
should, especially after deductions are made at the point of sale for
outstanding debts. An official estimate given by the NTB indicates
that in Tawang, not far from Bān Klāng in the same sub-district, the
average income of families in 1976 and 1978 was around M\$2,402 per
year, and returns from the sale of the tobacco harvest contributed
some M\$1,294 to the total household income (or more than 50 per
cent) (Teo 1979, pp. 10–11). In Bān Klāng a typical household
cultivates plots of land growing between 1,000 and 4,000 tobacco
plants, depending on the strength of labour force it has, which
should fetch between M\$1,000 and M\$1,500 per season. Some
households in Bān Klāng cultivate very extensively; one household in
particular netted approximately M\$14,000 in 1982. This was possible
because the head of the household had many grown-up children.
Although most were married and were then living outside the village,
they returned to Bān Klāng to help out in the field throughout the
growing season.

As mentioned above, the traditional economy of Bān Klāng was rice-growing and some market-gardening. There had also been other occupations as well. Firth notes that the Siamese used to make tiles in the 1940s and some also worked as plasterers and builders.[13] Nowadays no tile-manufacturing takes place in the village, although plastering and construction work continue to be associated with the Siamese, who have always been noted for their fine workmanship. Many Siamese men with this skill find temporary and permanent employment in the construction industry in various places in Kelantan.

Although there is no uniform pattern of employment, a typical household in Bān Klāng usually has some of its members, especially the younger ones, employed in various occupations outside the village while other members of the same household, particularly the parents, concentrate on tobacco-growing. Many people find urban employment working for the Chinese, especially as assistants in motor workshops, retail shops, supermarkets, hairdressing salons, tailoring shops, and factories. Siamese girls are often employed as domestic servants by Chinese families in the town. Many of these Chinese also have long-established relationships with the residents of Bān Klāng either through kin connection or through friendship.

In Bān Klāng, ninety-five households out of 126 have listed tobacco-growing as their chief occupation (Table 2.3). Because of the dominance of the tobacco industry, there is a tendency for most households to overemphasize their dependence on tobacco even when other members of the same household, including the head, bring in additional income from secondary jobs. As there is quite a long break between tobacco-growing seasons, many heads of households are involved in other occupations to supplement their income: six work full-time as carpenters and housebuilders outside the tobacco-growing season; three others run retail shops but let their wives and children look after the business during peak growing period. There are also two heads of households who work part-time as petty traders and one who operates a pirate taxi service. There are five people in the village who practise traditional healing and curing, also on a part-time basis. Six heads of households claim that they do various jobs around the village. Altogether twenty-four heads of households have secondary occupations to supplement their income from tobacco-growing. There are six heads of households whose main occupation is not agricultural. These are two taxi and van drivers, two housebuilders or carpenters, one school teacher, one store keeper, and one traditional medical specialist (*māu*; Malay: *bomoh*). Despite this, others in the same household are involved in tobacco-growing. Thus while the two drivers may be working outside the village, their wives and older children cultivate plots of tobacco. The same applies to the two carpenters and the school teacher. The full-time specialist in traditional medicine (*māu*) lives by himself and grows no tobacco but rents out his land to Malay tenants from a neighbouring village.

Table 2.3 also shows that sixteen households do not specify any particular occupation but their livelihood depends on the income of absentee members, typically children and relatives working outside the village. These households mainly consist of elderly men and women past their working age but who occasionally keep themselves busy helping out in the tobacco fields of friends and relatives. If they own land in the village they usually let their married children of separately established households work on it; some rent out their land to others. Between tobacco-growing seasons these semi-retired residents can be found spending most of their time at the temple.

TABLE 2.3
Primary Occupation of Heads
of Households in Bān Klāng

Occupation	No. of Heads of Households
Tobacco-growing	95
Housebuilder/carpenter	2
Retail shop owner	3
Coffee shop operator	2
Taxi/van driver	2
Tailor	1
School teacher	1
Store keeper	1
Furniture factory owner	1
Tobacco-processing plant owner	1
Dependent on absentee members	16
Bomoh (traditional medical specialist)	1
Total	126

As already mentioned, some members of households work and stay outside the village but they send money back regularly to supplement the household income. There are also household members who reside in Bān Klāng but work elsewhere outside the village; these include nine people who work as assistants in motor workshops, two shop assistants, one taxi driver and one van driver, two sawmill workers, and three housebuilders. It may appear that only a small fraction of the village population really work outside the village. But my census figures do not include those who have migrated temporarily to their workplaces, remaining there for most part of the year, but returning regularly to Bān Klāng for various reasons. The number who do so is considerable but difficult to estimate. What is really significant about these people is that they normally consider Bān Klāng their "home" village, which they identify with and express and maintain their emotional attachment through participation in its social and cultural activities. Their regular return to Bān Klāng during major temple celebrations makes the population of the village at such times more than double its usual size. Therefore, the census figures that I have regarding Bān Klāng residents at normal times of the year certainly do not include the number of "absentee" members who ought to be considered in the actual strength of Bān Klāng's social and religious community. Members of the community who return regularly to this ancestral village also include those who have migrated and are settling in various parts of southern Thailand, particularly in the land settlement schemes (*nikhom*) in Narathiwat province.

Apart from the two tobacco-curing plants, there is a furniture-making factory, which is also owned by a Chinese family of the village. It employs between fourteen and thirty-two workers, mainly male relatives and friends of the owner. Some of the workers are employed only intermittently, hence the range in the number of people actually working there. This family business produces cheap and middle-range household furniture for sale through various outlets in the district as well as by some shops in Kota Bharu.

Although Bān Klāng is located near the sea (about 1 kilometre away), fishing has not been anyone's chief occupation. Occasionally, some people do net casting along the sea-shore if only for their own household consumption. In contrast, men in neighbouring Malay villages are deep-sea fishermen.

Apart from rice, pig-farming used to be carried out on a large scale in Bān Klāng. Older residents of the village recall the time when pig raising was a major occupation of Bān Klāng. The swine-fever of 1928, however, wiped out the entire pig population,[14] and ever since pig-farming has never recovered itself. The demise of the industry appeared to be one of the major factors contributing to the impoverished condition in Bān Klāng before commercial tobacco was introduced in the 1960s.

Other domestic animals are not economically important either. Some households do keep one or two heads of cattle, but seldom more than that, because during the tobacco season virtually every available hand is needed for the crop. Despite this, domestic animals do provide additional cash income to the household. Animals that grow up to a size that fetches a high selling price are quickly sold off to Malay traders for slaughter in the local market or for export to bigger towns in the country.[15] No water buffaloes or goats are raised in the village.

Another important aspect of Bān Klāng's economy deserves special mention here. An account of the economic history of any Siamese village in Kelantan is not really complete without some discussion of the involvement of the Siamese as well as some rural Chinese in a land resettlement scheme known as the *nikhom* project.[16] During the 1960s some families from Bān Klāng moved to the southern Thai province of Narathiwat, to participate in the Thai government-sponsored scheme. For the people of Bān Klāng the resettlement project was very tempting since the subsistence economy based solely on rice-cultivation could barely support its expanding population. Many but not all of those who joined the scheme were landless; a shortage of land in Bān Klāng thus contributed to the attractiveness of the scheme. Although most households in the village owned land, the income they derived from rice-growing was inadequate for their livelihood. Hence the problem of acute poverty.

Such was the economic condition of Bān Klāng during the 1960s that any venture that might alleviate poverty and ease the pressure on land appeared very attractive indeed. Quite a large number of families from other Siamese villages in Kelantan also took part in the *nikhom* project. Most of them ended up in what is now known as *Nikhom* Pattana, *Nikhom* Mae Luang, *Nikhom* Waeng, and *Nikhom* Kilo

Sām, in Narathiwat province. However, heavy floods in 1967, the worst in forty years in the area, forced many of them back to their original villages in Kelantan. Even so, a few families, those who had been really landless back in Kelantan, stayed put despite the serious damage to their property.[17]

From Bān Klāng fifteen families, mainly young couples, were reported to have joined the scheme. Each was given twenty-five *raj* of land to be cleared for rubber trees and another two *raj* for a house lot.[18] A grant of 12,000 baht was also given, issued in small instalments over an extended period to cover the purchase of farm equipment and building materials for the house, plus a daily food allowance of 5 baht per family.

The significance of the *nikhom* scheme is that it provided timely release from population pressure on village land and from extreme poverty. But the *nikhom*, despite its promise of land ownership, was never meant to be an easy pursuit. There was tremendous hardship experienced by those taking part in the land scheme. Upon arriving at the new settlement, participants were left entirely on their own to clear the jungle and build their houses. In addition, despite the living allowances given to them, many settlers found that occasionally they had to take breaks to work in Kelantan whenever food supplies ran low, thereby delaying considerably the work of clearing the forest. By the time they returned from their breaks the clearing was often overrun by secondary growth.[19] Since the settlement scheme called for hard work and required strong physical and emotional endurance, only those who were really in desperate need of land remained permanently in Thailand.

After the great flood of 1967, many of the original settlers lost their pioneering spirit and returned for good to their villages in Kelantan. By that time too, the commercial cultivation of tobacco had become an important source of income. Those who abandoned the *nikhom* scheme had few regrets about doing so: the timely introduction of tobacco in the 1960s bailed them out of their poverty.[20]

The *nikhom* scheme is mentioned here for another important reason. Some of those who participated in the scheme were also Chinese. At least two Chinese families originally of Bān Klāng have settled permanently in the *nikhom* scheme. Despite being Chinese, they managed to convince the Thai recruiting officials that they were just as Siamese as any other resident of Bān Klāng. Their fluency in the Siamese language and the fact that no one in Bān Klāng protested against their joining the land scheme testify to the extent of their assimilation into the Siamese community.

On the whole, Bān Klāng has undergone a complete transformation from a community of rice-growers to a village of tobacco-farmers. An important feature of the village is that it is no longer a collectivity of people tied to an agricultural occupation in the traditional sense. The commercialization of agriculture and the involvement of its residents in occupations associated with the larger economy external to the village may at first appear to have undermined the village community. The "floating" nature of its population adds even more to the transient nature of village life in Bān Klāng. However, as the next few chapters will demonstrate, the concept of community still persists among the residents despite the radical change brought about by a decline in the traditional economy of the village. The introduction of commercial tobacco has even further consolidated this community, as evidenced by the two tobacco companies of the village giving generous support to the temple. It appears that profit from the tobacco trade is "ploughed" back directly into the community in the form of merit-making by shareholders of both companies. In the wake of these changes the temple has become all the more important as a social and religious institution which continues to bind together the whole village, plus its "absentee" members, as a closely knit community. Such solidarity does in fact exist even though it manifests itself in an emphatically Siamese cultural form. This is despite the fact that the Chinese account for half of the population of the village and that the most influential individuals in Bān Klāng politically and economically, among them the headman, are also Chinese. Thus, it is through their participation in temple rituals and temple-based activities that the residents of Bān Klāng are able to identify themselves as members of the same community and proclaim a collective identity regardless of ethnicity.

NOTES

1. For instance, see Skinner (1965), Wyatt (1974), Mohamed (1974), Marriott (1916), Rentse (1934), and Rahmat Saripan (1979). On the role of Siam in the affairs of Kedah and Perlis, see Bonney (1971),

Sharom Ahmat (1971), Banks (1980), and Vella (1957).

2. In fact, there was even an attempt to exploit this situation during the Kelantan civil war of succession in 1839. One of the contenders for the throne, Tuan Senik, wrote to the royal court in Siam that Siamese people and monks in Kelantan were being ill-treated by his rival, Tuan Besar (Skinner 1965, pp. 37, 43). Apparently, Senik thought that he could thus influence Siamese authority against Tuan Besar. But nothing eventuated, for the Siamese were pragmatic in their dealings with the Malay states and "well able to separate political and economic interests from religious affairs" (personal communication from Cyril Skinner to writer in 1984). Nevertheless, the attempt made by Tuan Senik testifies to the fact that local rulers and chiefs considered Siamese settlers in Kelantan as a special group of people whose presence must at least be tolerated, if not properly accommodated. The account by Abdullah bin Abdul Kadir Munshi also mentions that it was customary for the Siamese king to be the last person to decide on the next successor to the throne of Kelantan in the event of a dispute (Abdullah 1960, p. 60; Kassim Ahmad 1960, p. 74; Klinkert 1889, p. 45).

3. Skinner (1965) gives a detailed account of how the internal rivalry for the state throne of Kelantan, which resulted in the civil war of 1839, was eventually put to an end by the direct involvement of Siam. For accounts by other writers, see Wyatt (1974) and Chan (1965, p. 159).

4. The habit of sending a tribute of gold and silver to Bangkok, in the shape of the controversial tree called *bunga mas* has been interpreted in various ways. While some writers insist that the *bunga mas* was sent as a mark of friendship, others argue that the gift was symbolic of the political submission of the Malay states to the Siamese. On this, see Khasnor Johan (1965/66), Ismail Bakti (1979), Cushman and Milner (1979), Gullick (1963), Wyatt (1974), Banks (1980), and Bonney (1971).

5. See Pepys (1916), Brown (1956), Baker (1939), and Sturrock (1912). Ismail (1989) has listed a number of words in the Kelantanese dialect borrowed from the Siamese language.

6. For an account of the *naklēng*, see, for instance, Johnston (1980) and Golomb (1978).

7. A form of Siamese dance-drama which used to be very common among the Siamese communities in Kelantan and southern Thailand; although it is performed in the Malay dialect of Kelantan its stories "relate the adventures of characters who are not recognizably Malay in origin, in circumstances which are often quite foreign to Malaya" (Sheppard

1959, p. 12). It was thought to have originated from the old Kingdom of Ligor dating back to AD 400. Although the ancient kingdom disappeared after about AD 1250, when the Siamese took control of the country, *manōrā* was kept alive in many Siamese villages, particularly when it is performed as part of temple functions. For further accounts of *manōrā*, see Ginsburg (1972), Nicolas (1924), Sheppard (1959, 1973), Ghulam-Sarwar Yousof (1982), and Kershaw (1982).

8. "Urban" area is defined here as a place with 10,000 people and more. See Government of Malaysia, *1980 Population and Housing Census of Malaysia* (1983) and Hirschman (1972, pp. 21, 23).

9. Apparently quite a number of people in Bān Klāng are familiar with the legend of the establishment of Semerak, indicating, as Kershaw suggests, a close link between Bān Klāng and Semerak Siamese.

10. See Chapter 3 on the arrangements for the daily sending of food to feed temple residents.

11. The discussion in this part is based mainly on Teo (1979).

12. In Bān Klāng there are elderly men and women (sometimes, well past their fifties) who live by themselves in a separate household even though they have children of their own living in the same village. They normally depend on handouts from their children, if they have any, or else from close relatives. During the tobacco-growing season they help out with the lighter chores in the field, and look after the younger children at home, as well as take over some of the domestic duties. After the harvest and sale of tobacco leaves, they are rewarded accordingly.

13. When Firth mentions briefly the presence of a Siamese community to the north of his village of study, he probably has Bān Klāng in mind. According to him the community, with a temple and seminary staffed by Buddhist monks, was involved in rice-cultivation, tile-making, plastering, and other construction work (Firth 1966, p. 69).

14. The plague that affected Bān Klāng was apparently the same one that hit the Chinese village of Mentuan, not far away. A report mentions that some 210 pigs in Mentuan were killed by the disease (Report submitted by Kota Bharu Veterinary Officer, 19 November 1928; Pasir Puteh District Office File no. 405/28, Arkib Negara Malaysia).

15. Winzeler (1981, p. 13) states that animals raised by the non-Muslim Chinese are not likely to be purchased by Malays for purposes of ritual slaughter, particularly to mark the end of fasting, and so forth. While this may be so in his area of study, this preference does not seem to apply in Bān Klāng. While in the field I often encountered Malay traders who scout around Bān Klāng regularly to purchase animals being sold

at prices agreeable to them. In Kelantan the trading of cattle and buffaloes and the sale of fresh beef are exclusively associated with the Malays. The main point is that while most of these animals are supplied by Malay peasants, quite a few have to come from non-Muslim Siamese and Chinese.

16. Kershaw (1969) gives a good account of the scheme and the motives behind the recruitment of Siamese peasants from Kelantan to participate in the project.

17. I must stress here that many who took part in the *nikhom* scheme were not actually landless — even though they claimed to be so in the presence of the Thai recruiting authorities — but rather owned small pieces of land. As the already low returns to rice-growing declined relative to those from other pursuits, rampant poverty among the villagers was aggravated. In a few cases the settlers were landless in relative rather than absolute terms; most settlers were young married couples with parents still surviving. On the deaths of the parents of either couple, some inherited landed property. As their lot has not improved much even after moving to the *nikhom*, the windfall from the inheritance gave them a valid excuse to return to Kelantan. The *nikhom* project provided a change from one type of economy to another: the settlers went to the *nikhom* not to grow rice but to cultivate rubber, which was considered one of the most lucrative pursuits during the 1960s. Typical of those settlers who already own some land is one Bān Klāng family that inherited some ancestral land but chose instead to sell it when they moved to the *nikhom*. Incidently this family is now one of the better-off in the settlement, which is not at all surprising, because proceeds from the land sale in Kelantan were re-invested in the family's rubber holdings in the *nikhom*.

18. *Raj* is the unit used to measure land in Thailand. One *raj* is equivalent to 0.16 hectares or 0.4 acres.

19. Occasional trips back to ancestral villages in Kelantan, which were initially planned for a few days, were often extended to a few months when some of the settlers needed to find work in order to have enough money to buy the next stock of supplies for use in the *nikhom*; the allowance given by the Thai authorities was barely adequate. One informant in Bān Klāng confirmed that during one break he continued to stay in the village for nearly a year and that, by the time he went back to the settlement, his clearing had already reverted to secondary jungle. Discouraged, he left the settlement and returned permanently to Bān Klāng, where he still owns some land.

20. As mentioned above, many of those who took part in the *nikhom* scheme were not really landless. Some people owned land, but whatever they used to get out of rice-growing was barely adequate to support a decent living; hence the *nikhom* scheme seemed to be a viable alternative under the circumstances. The introduction of commercial tobacco-farming, however, brought about a radical change in the economy of the village. Tobacco gives lucrative returns and greater profit compared with rice-farming. Thus many settlers who quit the *nikhom* returned to the village and benefited by growing tobacco on whatever land they owned.

Chapter 3
The Kelantanese Order of Monks

The twenty Buddhist temples in Kelantan collectively constitute a religious and social network which covers southern Thailand and northern Terengganu. However, if also included is the "export" of Kelantanese monks to staff temples in Singapore, Kuala Lumpur, and other places in the west coast states of peninsular Malaysia, the network covers a larger area. While most temples are located in Siamese villages, two are found in Chinese settlements, although the monks are Siamese. A number of Siamese villages that have no temples of their own often have some kind of building structures, such as a resting pavilion (*sālā phak song*) or monastic house, built to accommodate visiting monks who frequent these places to conduct various religious services, including merit-making and at times the ordination of candidates into novices.

Kelantanese temples are grouped under four religious districts, each headed by an abbot with the title of "District Religious Head" (*caw khana amphōe*).[1] In Tumpat administrative district, which is adjacent to the Siamese border, two positions of *caw khana amphōe* have been created because of the large number of temples. The temples in the administrative districts of Pasir Mas and Tanah Merah are placed under the responsibility of only one *caw khana amphōe*. Similarly, temples in the administrative districts of Bachok, Pasir Puteh, and Kota Bharu are grouped under one district religious head. At the top of the state Buddhist religious hierarchy is the Chief Monk (*caw khana rat*); his official Malay title is *Ketua Besar Sami Buddha Negeri Kelantan* (Figure 3.1).

The monks are referred to as *phra* by the Siamese, while Kelantan

Malays use the term *tok ca*. In standard Malay the term commonly
used, although etymologically incorrect, is *sami Buddha*, obviously
in resemblance to the original usage meant for priests of Hindu and
Chinese religions. The term *tok raja* in Kelantanese Malay dialect is
used to refer specifically to the abbot of a temple (*caw āwāt*). "Buddhist temple" is known in Kelantan Malay dialect as *ketik*, a word
which is suspected to originate from the Pāli *kuti* (the monks' living
cubicle); in standard Malay the word *kuil Buddha* is often used for
"temple", although it is also etymologically incorrect. There are also
other terms in the local dialect which refer to various Buddhist ritual
events: ordination is known as *masuk jadi tok ca, masuk pakai kain
kuning* (literally, "to don the yellow cloth"); merit-making (*thambun*)
is known as *membuat pahala*; and temple celebrations (*ngān wat*) are
generally known as *kerja ketik*. These Kelantanese Malay terms are
used by the Siamese themselves particularly when they have to com-
municate in the local dialect with others who do not understand the
Siamese language. Likewise, the terms also find their way into the
monastic circulars (*batchōen*), part of which is printed in the Malay
language, which announce forthcoming temple events.

Although Buddhism is not a state religion, high-ranking monks
of the Buddhist ecclesiastical organization in Kelantan receive some
kind of royal patronage from the state's Muslim ruler. Officially the
sultan of Kelantan is responsible, by tradition, for the confirmation
of appointments to important positions within the hierarchy of the
state *sangha*, including that of the Chief Monk, his deputy, and other
monks heading various districts, a procedure which gives effective
symbolic expression to the traditional structure of state-*sangha* power
relations. The sultan of Kelantan, who is the titular head of Islam,
thus also plays a role similar to that of the Thai monarch, that is, as
a protector of the Buddhist religion (*phutthasāsanupathampok*).[2]

Beyond this symbolic role, the state has little to do with the running of Buddhist temples and the choice of *sangha* leadership. The
sangha exists quite independently of the state in so far as financial
grants from the secular authority are concerned; its senior members
do not receive regular stipends from the government. This contrasts
with the case of Thailand where monks holding high offices receive
a state allowance, known as *nitayaphat*.[3] Nevertheless, occasional
grants are made to some temples in Kelantan by political parties or
the government, but these are usually acquired through the medi-

FIGURE 3.1
(a) Organization of the Kelantan *Sangha* in 1987

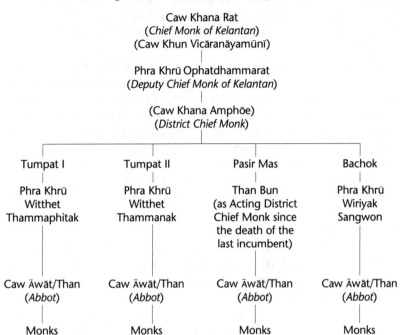

Caw Khana Rat
(*Chief Monk of Kelantan*)
(Caw Khun Vicāranāyamūnī)

Phra Khrū Ophatdhammarat
(*Deputy Chief Monk of Kelantan*)

(Caw Khana Amphōe)
(*District Chief Monk*)

Tumpat I	Tumpat II	Pasir Mas	Bachok
Phra Khrū Witthet Thammaphitak	Phra Khrū Witthet Thammanak	Than Bun (as Acting District Chief Monk since the death of the last incumbent)	Phra Khrū Wiriyak Sangwon
Caw Āwāt/Than (*Abbot*)	Caw Āwāt/Than (*Abbot*)	Caw Āwāt/Than (*Abbot*)	Caw Āwāt/Than (*Abbot*)
Monks	Monks	Monks	Monks

(b) Distribution of Temples According to District in 1987

Tumpat I — Phikhunthāung (6), Cāēngputthāwāt (5), Majsuwankhīrī (7), Chonphrachumthāt (5), and Khōgsiyā (5)

Total number of monks in the district — 28

Tumpat II — Sukhauntārām (1), Matchimārām (6), Prachumtātchonārām (5), Phikhunjaj (7), and Tawā (5)

Total number of monks in the district — 24

Pasir Mas — Prachācīnārām (5), Pōthitwihān (7), Cīnpradittharām (5), Uttamārām (10), Champākaew (8), and Khōsakārām (0)

Total number of monks in the district — 35

Bachok and — Pathumwihān (6), Phutthaksinmingmongkhon (9),
Pasir Puteh Majprachāsāmagkhī (0), and Ariyakīrī (1)

Total number of monks in the district — 16

Total number of monks in the state — 103

NOTE: Numbers within parentheses indicate number of monks for each temple.

ation of the Chinese. Another benefit enjoyed by the Kelantanese *sangha* is exemption from paying taxes on temple lands since they are always classified as reserves for mosques and cemeteries (*tanah wakaf*).

As temples do not receive regular government grants, they have to find their own sources of funding. Although most temples are adequately provided with a daily supply of cooked food to maintain the monastic residents, to meet their other expenses they have to depend on regular donations of money and goods from the general public, including the residents of the village in which the temple is located as well as outsiders from places far afield. Sometimes money is also raised by holding special functions (*ngān hā bia*) during which appeals are made to as many of the Buddhist population as possible. As a rule the larger is the number of its suporters the better is the temple financially.

A close relationship exists between temples in Kelantan and those in Thailand, and this is crucial to the survival of the religion in more ways than one. Thailand and its *sangha* have always been the source of religious and cultural tradition for Kelantanese temples. Despite the fact that Siamese in Kelantan, in close association with their temples, are known to adhere to additional beliefs and ritual practices which are specific to this region, they also keep a close watch on the latest development in the practice and propagation of Buddhism in Thailand, and innovative ideas from across the border are often imported and quickly adapted to local usage. Emulating the Thai *sangha* in many of its ritual and organizational aspects, the Kelantanese *sangha* also judges its own purity of practice and tradition by reference to its Thai counterpart. One way of ensuring this is through religious examinations based on the Thai curriculum. For this purpose, representatives of the Thai ecclesiastical authority travel annually to a temple in Tumpat district to conduct and supervise these examinations. Those wishing to pursue higher studies in Buddhist learning are encouraged to do so in Thailand. Monks who aspire to serve for an extended period of time not only have to sit for these examinations; they are also expected to spend some time in Thailand in order to acquire the necessary exposure to the more sophisticated religious learning and teaching, and to practise monastic discipline, including meditation. Therefore a sojourn or two in Thailand is highly valued as part of a monk's resumé, perhaps making it look more impressive and authentic. In fact, many of the more senior monks and abbots now serving in Kelantan have spent the earlier period of their monkhood studying under various monastic teachers in Thailand.

Exchanges of visits between Kelantanese and Thai monks also take place regularly. A common practice is to invite distinguished monks from Thailand to participate as honoured guests or as titular patrons (*phū upatham*) in major ceremonies; more often than not they are also asked to deliver special sermons for the occasion. Other visiting monks and laymen from Thailand also demonstrate the finer techniques of performing rituals and the proper way of conducting certain ceremonies; these are expected to be emulated by Kelantanese monks and the local Buddhist population. Invitation to attend temple ceremonies in Kelantan is not limited to monks alone. Nuns (*māechī*) from Thailand are often invited to grace these occasions.

The close link between the *sangha* of Kelantan and that of Thailand testifies to one important aspect of this study. Most of those monks who are actively involved in monastic activities are ethnically Siamese. For instance, Kelantanese candidates for the religious examinations and monks who travel to Thailand for a visit or study are mostly Siamese. Hence, it is Siamese monks who are responsible for maintaining the vital link between the *sangha* bodies of Thailand and Kelantan.

Kelantanese monks often receive some of the privileges customarily accorded to monks in Thailand; in fact, Kelantanese monks tend to enjoy better benefits in Thailand than they would have received in their own home state. Among these are exemption from hospital fees and admission to first-class wards, privileges commonly granted to Thai monks.[4] Other benefits include special facilities extended to travelling monks at Thai customs and immigration check-points. Travel concessions given to Thai monks on public transportation are also enjoyed by Kelantanese monks whenever they visit Thailand.

The close relationship between the Thai and the Kelantanese *sangha* is also expressed in ceremonial form. The chief monk and, occasionally, district heads of temples receive ceremonial fans (*phat jot*) from Thailand as a token of their religious and ceremonial dependence on the Thai *sangha*. The Kelantanese *sangha* thus maintains a dualistic existence. While the fans given by the Thai *sangha* symbolize the close relationship between the Kelantanese *sangha* and the Thai *sangha*, the letters of appointments from the sultan symbolize the patronage of a Malay ruler. Its position is validated by Thai ecclesiastical authority and Malay political authority simultaneously.

Despite its close relationship with the *sangha* of Thailand, the Kelantanese *sangha* is beset with a crucial problem: the declining number of males who are prepared to become full-time monks. This misfortune befalls nearly all Kelantanese temples. By Thai standard, the average monastic population per temple in Kelantan is very small.[5] In many cases the number of monks of a particular temple is hardly enough to maintain the quorum (*song*) necessary for the proper conduct of rituals.[6] Hence it is most common for resident monks of various temples to join forces to make up for the number by attending monastic functions in other villages. In addition redistributions of the monk population are organized, often initiated by the layman committee of a village whose temple has an insufficient number of monks. Hence, many monks change their residence, moving from a temple with a "surplus" to another that has less than the required minimum.

The *sangha*, realizing that there are now fewer people interested in becoming monks particularly for an extended period of time, has to make do with a dwindling number of monks. Some temples have no alternative but to close down temporarily because the number of monks available, despite efforts at redistributing them to where they are badly needed, is hardly adequate to maintain them. For instance, the second temple in Bān Klāng has been left unoccupied for a number of years (except for the occasional return of a monk during the day). Another temple in Kok Kho village, in Pasir Mas district, was closed down in 1982 because its abbot had decided to disrobe in order to follow a more worldly pursuit as a traditional medical practitioner. However, in 1983 the same temple was re-opened when monks from Kubang Panjang decided to move in, but at the expense of the temple in Kubang Panjang, which was then closed down.

Surprisingly, the dwindling number of monks does not mean that there are now fewer ordination ceremonies being held in most temples. In fact, ordinations are numerous but few of those ordained remain monks for a prolonged period. Hence the reduced number of monks serving for a longer period in the *sangha*. In practice there

TABLE 3.1
Population of Temples in Kelantan

Temple Name	Number of Monks in			
	1976	1978	1982	1983
1. Tawā	5	6	6 (1)	5
2. Matchimārām	5	7	5	5
3. Phikhunjaj	5	10	5	7
4. Prachumtātchonārām	5	6 (1)	5	6
5. Sukhauntārām	5	5	4	0
6. Phikhunthaung	8	11	8 (1)	9
7. Cāēngputthāwāt	8	7 (3)	9 (3)	7
8. Khōgsiyā	5	5	5	6
9. Chonphracumthāt	5	6	6	5
10. Majsuwankhīrī	8	9	7	9
11. Pōthitwihān	8	8	6	5
12. Majprachāsāmagkhī	0	5 (2)	0	0
13. Pathumwihān	6	6	6	5 (1)
14. Khōsakārām	4	7	0	5
15. Uttamārām	7	8	6	6
16. Ariyakīrī	4	9	5 (1)	5
17. Champākaew	5	11 (2)	8	6
18. Phutthaksinmingmongkhon	5	10	5	5
19. Cīnpraditthārām	5	0	5	5
20. Prachācīnārām	6	6	5	6
Total	109	142 (8)	106 (6)	107 (1)
Average number of monks per temple	5.5	7.1	5.3	5.4

NOTE: Numbers within parentheses indicate number of novices.
SOURCE: Deputy Chief Abbot of Kelantan, Wat Prachācīnārām, Wakaf Baru.

are two types of ordination ceremonies: short-term and long-term. Short-term initiates remain monks for a few days, usually seven, sometimes even fewer days. Their ordination is mainly for the purpose of fulfilling vows or making merit for deceased members of the family. Golomb refers to this type as "token ordination", and applies the term to any stay as monks of three or fewer months (Golomb 1978, p. 132). This type of ordination is more prevalent among the rural Chinese of Kelantan; as a norm Siamese families rarely organize it.[7] Because of the motives involved, the short-term ordination is commonly known as *buat bon*, meaning "ordination for the purpose of fulfilling a vow" (Kershaw 1981, p. 82). The ceremonies for short-term ordinations are as just as elaborate, and perhaps as costly, as those for long-term ones, except that candidates are not expected to memorize all the lines in Pali they have to say during the ceremonies. They merely have to repeat every word after the ordaining monks.

Ordination for a longer period usually requires the initiates to study beforehand the procedure of ordination and acquire the basic knowledge of monastic rules. Since they are expected to be monks for longer than the token period, their ordination is viewed as a very serious undertaking by all parties involved. A stay of at least one year is usual for the second type of ordination, but there is no guarantee that the newly ordained monk will remain permanently in the *sangha*. There is always the possibility of the young monk, even the most promising ones, disrobing at any time for various reasons, including career opportunities in more worldly pursuits.[8]

To ensure that the ordained remain in the *sangha* for a reasonable period the Kelantanese *sangha* at its 1981 meeting decided on a ruling which requires that a new monk should serve a minimum of three years after being ordained. The rationale for this is that if a person were to leave the *sangha* within the first one or two years after ordination, the experience that he had acquired would not justify the considerable cost of his ordination. Apparently, the *sangha* is of the opinion that three years is the minimum necessary for a person to become competent to continue conducting Buddhist rituals after his return to lay life. Whether this ruling will work is yet to be seen, for a precedent of this nature has never been set even in Thailand itself. However, the general feeling among the Kelantan Siamese is that this ruling is justified and acceptable as a measure to maintain the state's monk population at an adequate level.

The same ruling, however, does not apply to short-term type of ordination. The majority of those who are ordained in this manner are people who want to make merit and who would never consider a long-term commitment in the monkhood. "Token ordinations" are conducted frequently irrespective of the three years' ruling, since the temples involved will benefit from the contributions of money and gifts. As this has always been a traditional source of revenues, any attempt to discourage this kind of ordination would disadvantage the temples financially.

Ordination, Cultural Behaviour, and Ethnicity

Swearer argues that in Thailand monastic training is the key to the profound attitude of respect that the *sangha* gains from the community at large. At the same time, ordination into the *sangha* raises the status of an ordinary man, for "having been a member of the *sangha* is perceived to be as a good in and of itself" (Swearer 1976*a*, p. 27). Tambiah points out that ordination *per se* is socially and religiously significant:

> If ordination to monkhood is in religious terms a rite of initiation, in social terms it is distinctively a rite of passage for young men before they marry and set up their own households. (Tambiah 1970, p. 101)

Bunnag emphasizes that monkhood accords great advantages in terms of increased prestige, as well as other tangible benefits (Bunnag 1973, p. 43). The same can also be said about ordination in Kelantan. For instance, the change of status is almost immediately recognized by fellow villagers. At the very least an ordained person who returns to lay life after a spell in the *sangha* can expect to have the prefix to his name changed from *eh* to *chaw*, a kind of social indicator that distinguishes the "initiated" from those who are not. The new name that an ordained person is given elevates him to a new status where he remains for the rest of his life. As a contrast, an unordained man is referred to as an "immature" or "uncooked" person (*khon dib*). Hence monkhood, highly valued and culturally desirable, marks the transition from boyhood to adulthood. The titles of respect are also extended to the parents of a serving monk. They should be rightfully addressed by honorific titles of *jāum phūchāj* for the father, and *jāum phūjing* for the mother.

Entrance into the monkhood is not so much in quest of *nirvana* but to make merit for oneself and one's parents. By taking the yellow robe, a person accumulates merit, of which a good portion is believed to benefit the parents of the ordained candidate. This belief is further strengthened by the parents themselves, who feel that their life is incomplete unless they have received merit by having their sons ordained as monks (Klausner 1964, p. 72). Social pressure is often the reason for taking the yellow robe, especially in the case of temporary ordinations (cf. Kaufman 1960, p. 120).

Apart from the question of merit accumulation, monastic life has practical benefit, for being ordained expands one's sphere of orientation. One is exposed to the network of temples and religious organization that extends well beyond the village — usually into Thailand and also into other parts of the country. Chances to travel are enhanced during one's ordained life; it is common for monks to be invited by patrons from distant places, with travel expenses fully met by the hosts. Chances of establishing contacts with people who come to the temple to make merit tend to improve the longer the time one spends in the *sangha.* These contacts often prove to be advantageous should the monk subsequently return to lay life.[9]

Apart from that, persons who have been ordained for some time, especially the younger, come across opportunities to learn a new trade and skills, such as in the building and construction business. For instance, in Thailand newly ordained monks can learn from their abbots and the elder monks a large range of skills covering architecture, carpentry, sculpture, painting and decorative art, bronze-casting, tile-, brick-, and cement-making, and traditional medicine (cf. Klausner 1964, p. 74). Kelantanese monks who stay in temples for an extended period often pick up valuable trade skills, although the range may not be very extensive. Yet the opportunity to acquire new skills is always there for those with a genuine interest. Most temples in Kelantan have at some time a variety of projects going on, mainly to construct new buildings or to renovate existing ones. If adequate fund is available hired labour is used, otherwise the younger monks and novices are expected to shoulder the greater part of the work themselves with voluntary help from the villagers. At least part of the labour cost is thus defrayed by the monks themselves. It is not uncommon to see monks and novices engaged in bricklaying, carpentry, and masonry. For those who have been construction workers prior to ordination, the further acquisition of such skills is especially useful. Some Kelantanese temples are noted for monks who specialize in traditional healing and herbal medicine; younger monks who reside at this temple often pick up this knowledge as well. These are among the skills which any newly ordained monk could easily learn, but most significantly, the monastic environment has the capacity to provide training and to prepare monks for employment in the secular world once they leave the *sangha.*

A most important feature of involvement in the monkhood in Thailand is that it starts early in one's life. De Young observes that there is usually a gradual progression in the stages of a person's association with the monastic institution, beginning from a temple boy (*dek wat*), to a novice (*nēn*), and finally to a fully ordained monk (De Young 1966, p. 117).

Such a path is by no means typical of Kelantanese monks. In fact, the institution of temple boys has not been practised for a long time. Most Siamese children are likely to attend formal schooling in the neighbouring Malay villages. Furthermore, very few men become novices for a stipulated period prior to ordination, as used to be the case in the old days. In fact, there is now a tendency to do away with the lengthy and gradual stages of admission into the monastic life. In the ideal situation one should first become a novice for a considerable period in order to acquire the necessary knowledge of the Buddhist doctrine and the skill to read Pali scriptures. Prospective monks are expected to learn about the monastic rules (*phra winaj*) beforehand; from close association with the clergy they should pick up informally as much religious knowledge as possible. Once ordained, they intensify their understanding of the monastic rules and Buddhist teachings by learning from texts and by receiving formal instructions from more senior monks. However, this ideal of pre-ordination association with the temple is increasingly difficult to attain, partly because many youths are employed outside the village, returning only mostly during the weekends, while younger children attend formal schooling full time. As a result their personal and informal contact with the clergy has been greatly reduced. Gone are the days when candidates resided at the temples for months or even years on end to learn the monastic rules as a preparation for their ordination.

Most ordinations in Kelantan today take an abbreviated form; the case is especially obvious during "token" ordinations. Two separate ceremonies are often compressed into one single day; ordination of candidates as novices is conducted in the morning, while ordination into monkhood takes place almost immediately in the afternoon. Thus within the span of a single day one changes status from layman to novice and then to monk, whereas in the ideal case the process is spread out over many years. Furthermore, a "token" candidate does not normally go to any great lengths to prepare himself, because his stay in the *sangha* will not last more than a few days.

Even in the ordination ceremony for monks intended for a long-term stay, in which a candidate is supposed to learn his lines by heart, it is quite common for him to be prompted occasionally by the officiating monks (*khū suat*). At first it appears that the candidate is ill-prepared for the ceremony, but this stance is considered quite normal by most people. Even after being ordained, such a person does not normally devote his short-term stay to acquiring the necessary knowledge associated with Buddhism. He often has to be prompted in any chanting that he has to do or any utterance, even of basic formulae. More often than not, other senior monks, to whose care the newly ordained candidate is entrusted, often said it on his behalf. The lack of prior preparation for monkhood becomes obvious when many junior monks appear to be incompetent even in the procedures of conducting simple Buddhist rites.[10]

In Bān Klāng ordination is considered socially important, at least in so far as it concerns the Siamese half of the population. Most of the Siamese heads of households have been ordained at some stage in their lives, the majority before marriage. In contrast, a large proportion of the Chinese heads of households remain unordained. This discrepancy in the ordination status between Siamese and Chinese males also seems quite common in other parts of Kelantan. Ordination into the monkhood has never been a Chinese ethnic characteristic, even though the Chinese public, especially those of *Cina kampung* category, appear to be ardent supporters of Siamese temples, particularly with regard to meeting the material needs of monastic institution. Simply stated, a Siamese adult male is most likely to have been ordained, perhaps for one year or more, whereas a Chinese male of the same age-group may not have been at all. Even if a Chinese male has been ordained, the probability is high that the ordination which he has undergone will be of the "token" type.

The tradition of ordination is upheld by the Siamese even if it means having to cut short the length of one's stay in the *sangha*. Kershaw observes that there had been a decline in the number of ordinations in the last twenty years in Kelantan, but the Siamese still insist on male ordination (Kershaw 1981, p. 92, fn. 43). Concerted efforts are constantly being made to uphold the tradition, even if some compromises have to be made. As for the Chinese, ordination is not a matter of great concern, except perhaps for the purpose of fulfilling a vow or for some other pragmatic reasons.

Thus, the general pattern of ordination is that Siamese candidates tend to spend more time as monks than their Chinese counterparts. While short-term Chinese monks are numerous, full-time ones appear to be less common. For example, Kershaw points out that during 1974, there were only three Chinese who were in the *sangha* for reasons other than "token ordination"; two of these were abbots (ibid.). Presumably these were the only Chinese who have committed themselves to being monks for a long-term period, which in Kelantan appears to be the exception rather than the rule.

The case of Bān Klāng illustrates that there is a higher incidence of ordination among the Siamese than the Chinese (see Table 3.2). There are ninety-five male heads of households in the village; out of the ninety-five households, forty-five are headed by Siamese men, all but one of whom have been ordained. In contrast, the remaining fifty households are headed by Chinese males, of whom only sixteen have been ordained. Thus 98 per cent of Siamese male heads of households have been ordained, as compared with 32 per cent of Chinese ones.

The percentage of ordination for all heads of households in Bān Klāng is 63 per cent. In comparison, Kaufman estimated that 80 per cent of men between the ages of twenty-one and thirty in a community he studied, where the majority of the population was Thai, had joined the monkhood for at least one year (Kaufman 1960, p. 148). Although I have no comparable quantified data for individuals of this age-group, Siamese youths in Bān Klāng are more likely to have been ordained at some stage in their lives than Chinese youths of the same village; if ordained, the Siamese tend to stay ordained longer than their Chinese counterparts. They are also more likely to be ordained at an earlier age compared with Chinese of the same age-

TABLE 3.2
Ordination Status of Heads of Households in Bān Klāng

	Siamese	Chinese	All
Unordained	1 (2.2%)	34 (68.0%)	35 (36.8%)
Ordained	44 (97.8%)	16 (32.0%)	60 (63.2%)
Total	45	50	95

group. Kershaw's statement above lends support to this observation.

Table 3.3 records the length of time that ordained men have spent as monks. The "token" type of ordination (of three to seven days) is more prevalent among the Chinese, accounting for six out of seven cases, while there is only one case among the Siamese. There are fifty-three cases of long-term ordinations; the Chinese accounting for only ten of these, the Siamese forty-three.

The longest period of ordination for a household head, of the duration of nine Lents,[11] is that of a Chinese. The longest period of ordination for a Siamese household head is eight Lents. However, among all ordained persons in the village, the longest period of ordination is ten Lents: that of a Siamese who is not a household

TABLE 3.3
Time Spent as Ordained Monks by Heads of Households

	Siamese		Chinese		All	
Short-term						
3 days	1	(2.3%)	2	(12.5%)	3	(5.0%)
7 days	—		4	(25.0%)	4	(6.7%)
Long-term						
1 Lent	15	(34.1%)	4	(25.0%)	19	(31.7%)
2 Lents	10	(22.7%)	1	(6.3%)	11	(18.3%)
3 Lents	9	(20.5%)	2	(12.5%)	11	(18.3%)
4 Lents	1	(2.3%)	1	(6.3%)	2	(3.3%)
5 Lents	4	(9.1%)	—		4	(6.7%)
6 Lents	3	(6.8%)	—		3	(5.0%)
7 Lents	—		—		—	
8 Lents	1	(2.3%)	1	(6.3%)	2	(3.3%)
9 Lents	—		1	(6.3%)	1	(1.7%)
Total number of heads of households ordained	44		16		60	
Number of heads of households ordained for short-term duration	1		6		7	
Number of heads of households ordained for long-term duration	43		10		53	

head, and hence not listed in Table 3.3. However, the length of ordination period may not necessarily be indicative of an individual's commitment to the Buddhist religion. As will be seen, length of one's ordination may have no correlation with or direct bearing upon active involvement in temple affairs.

As mentioned, the Siamese normally view monkhood as a duty demanded of a good Buddhist. To be ordained is an important part of a man's life, in keeping with the universal Thai tradition. However, ordination alone is not enough since one should spend sufficient time in the *sangha* in order to gain monastic experience and understanding of the Buddhist religion. Hence, the Siamese consider "token ordination" (*buat bon*) as far from ideal cultural behaviour.

Apart from the contrasting emphasis placed on ordination by the Siamese and the Chinese, another important difference concerns the relationship between ex-monks and the temple where they have spent most of their ordained life. Ideally, an ex-monk should always maintain a good relationship with his host temple by returning to it regularly during its major functions and by participating in its rituals. This expectation is not that difficult to fulfil, particularly if the temple is located in the same village where he lives or within its immediate neighbourhood.

Most Siamese ex-monks make the effort to maintain this kind of post-ordination relationship. In contrast, many Chinese ex-monks do not regularly return to participate in the rituals held at their former temples. This may be partly explained by the fact that some live in other villages or in towns. However, among Bān Klāng residents there is a considerable number of Chinese ex-monks who tend to shy away from temple rituals. They include the longest-ordained ex-monk who appears to have the least interest in temple affairs. In view of his long period as a monk, he should have been a member of the temple steering committee (*sangkhārī*). Far from it, he does not even seem to be attending temple rituals regularly.

The following case illustrates the same kind of relationship between Chinese ex-monks and their former temples of ordination. During my field-work in 1982 and 1983 two Chinese were ordained, one for a period of seven days, the other for three. Yet after disrobing neither was to be seen again at the temple except occasionally at major functions. Even then, they attend merely as observers rather than as involved participants. Apparently they did not even go through the ritual procedure of receiving the vow of the five precepts, an important prelude associated with most Buddhist rituals. Instead they remained outside the sermon hall quite indifferent to the ritual progress going on inside. One might have expected former monks to be more involved in temple affairs. Yet there is nothing abnormal in the way these ex-monks are behaving; Chinese ex-monks are noted for their minimal participation in temple rituals. Nor are they even expected to assume the role of lay ritual leaders, mainly because they have limited knowledge of the technicalities of Buddhist rituals. This is understandable because during the brief period of ordination there was very little opportunity to learn about ritual procedures and delve deeper into the Theravāda Buddhist religion, partly because the corpus of the liturgy is in formal and written Thai.

These two Chinese ex-monks appeared to be of the opinion that they had performed their obligations as good Buddhists simply by having become monks, however briefly. They even talked with fondness and nostalgia about their sojourn as monks, but did not seem to be bothered by the fact that they rarely returned to participate in temple rituals. This behaviour contrasts with that of their wives and mothers, who go to the temple more often than do the ex-monks themselves.

It appears that women of both Siamese and Chinese households constitute the majority of those who attend the temple. If not for them the number of participants would be quite small, save for a few Siamese men who sit on the temple's committee (*sangkhārī*) and a handful of other Siamese laymen. It also appears that while most Chinese households in the village are represented only by their women in temple celebrations, it is most common for many Siamese households to be represented by both male and female household members during these occasions. In general, Chinese households are involved in temple affairs in two ways; while the male members contribute financially to temple funds but normally choose not to participate in temple rites, their female counterparts provide labour and participate in temple celebrations. In contrast, male members of Siamese households contribute both labour and money, and at the same time participate in temple rites to a degree far greater than do male Chinese household members.

The fundamental differences between a Siamese ex-monk and a Chinese ex-monk should be clear. A Siamese who has disrobed usually maintains his association with the temple in various ways, which manifests his staunch loyalty and devotion to the institution. If he happens to live outside the village in which the temple is located, he is verly likely to return at least during major ceremonies. However, in most cases even ordinary ceremonies will see him and his family returning to the village. There is, therefore, a continuity in the sense that his association with the temple does not end when he returns to lay life. Certainly a change of status is involved here — from an unordained person to a novice, to a monk, and finally to an ordained layman — but definitely there is no abrupt discontinuity in his familiar relationship with the temple. In fact, his acquaintance and familiarity with the temple starts well before he is ordained. Part of his socialization begins at a tender age as he accompanies his parents to the temple. As he matures he learns to pay appropriate respect to the monks. When asked to do chores for the monks he duly obeys without question. He passes through a whole series of transformations as part of his social upbringing — from a young child who frequents the temple at every possible occasion, to a youth who helps with work around the temple, to a monk, and finally to an ex-monk. His association with the temple should continue until the later years of his life. On his death he is likely to be cremated at the temple. His whole life from the beginning to the end therefore revolves around the temple.

In contrast, Chinese ex-monks in Kelantan rarely associate themselves with Buddhist temples in the same manner and degree. Even in Bān Klāng, where the Chinese constitute more than half of the population, there is a certain distance in the relationship between Chinese ex-monks and the temple. For instance, leading roles in rituals seem always the preserve of Siamese ex-monks, particularly members of the temple's steering committee. Important decisions regarding temple affairs that involve the interest of the public are deliberated by members of the steering committee, all but one of whom are Siamese. While some Chinese men do attend temple gatherings, they do so only as uninvolved participants or casual observers. However, it would be wrong to conclude that this is because the majority of the Chinese household heads have not been ordained, or have been through "token" ordinations only. On the contrary, in Bān Klāng there are quite a number of Chinese who have been ordained for a relatively long period. However, as a general rule

Chinese ex-monks display little interest in attending temple rites except for the major ones.

What really matters, therefore, is not only how long one has been ordained but also what happens after one has returned to lay life. Whether one continues to associate oneself with the temple or whether one keeps away from it is the crucial factor that distinguishes Chinese from Siamese supporters of the temple: how the relationship of a period of ordination to the total life-cycle is differently seen by village Siamese and Chinese in Kelantan. This contrast is crucial for understanding how the Siamese of Bān Klāng define their ethnic identity by reference to Buddhism and the commitment they have towards the religion and its temple tradition, even though most Chinese in the village also consider themselves Buddhists and members of the temple's congregation.

With regard to women's participation in temple affairs, one notices that despite the fact that they constitute the larger proportion of temple attendance, they do not become members of the *sangha*. Two women, however, have become "nuns" (*māechī*). But *māechī*, by definition, are not members of the *sangha* because they do not go through the ordination procedures of the monks. Nor do women sit on the lay committee of the temple (*sangkhārī*). To this extent women are excluded from religious power and prestige, since sacerdotal and ritual knowledge is the prerogative of the all-male *sangkhārī* members and monks. Yet, women seem to be very important, and at times indispensable, as ritual participants and as a source of labour. They prepare food daily to feed the monks, while during temple celebrations they help with the preparation of festive food and other work associated with the function. Although women's role regarding temple affairs is supportive, they may be a force to be reckoned with in behind-the-scene temple politics.

Two main points regarding the general perception of ethnicity and cultural behaviour should be noted here. First, the Siamese perception of and commitment to Theravāda Buddhism differ in many ways from those of the Chinese. For the former, Theravāda Buddhism is the *sine qua non* of being Siamese; it underlies Siamese ethnic identity. Siamese therefore place a different emphasis on the importance of Buddhist rituals and ceremonies than do the Chinese. For instance, while ordination into the monkhood is considered crucial by the Siamese, for the Chinese this is not necessarily so. Attendance at temple rituals also indicates that the Siamese are more committed to the religion: the more devout Siamese make an effort to attend even minor ceremonies while the Chinese are more inclined to be present only at the larger ones.

Second, it is the Siamese who play the crucial role in most Buddhist religious affairs. Hence, they constitute almost the entire membership of the Kelantanese Order of Monks. At the village level it is also the Siamese who play the leading role in temple organization. The next few chapters will show that even in a village like Bān Klāng, where there is a large Chinese population, laymen who are actively involved in temple affairs are mostly Siamese. Whereas the Chinese as an ethnic category are noted for their generosity in sponsoring many temple ceremonies and in providing material support to the temple, they neither run monastic affairs nor involve themselves in the monkhood on a long-term basis.

NOTES

1. These religious districts do not necessarily coincide with government administrative districts (Malay: *jajahan*). For the distribution of the monastic population according to temples in Kelantan, see Table 3.1.

2. On the relevance of this concept to the structure of relationship between Buddhism and the state, see the discussion in Ishii (1986).

3. Bunnag mentions that the *nitayaphat* allowance is an essential part of state support for the *sangha* in the sense that it provides a regular financial allowance to monks who are too tied up to official duties to go on the morning rounds of collecting alms food (*pajbinthabāt*) (Bunnag 1973, p. 61); see also Ishii (1986, p. 75).

4. Kelantanese monks prefer to go to hospitals in Thailand because their staff members are knowledgeable in monastic discipline. For example, the prohibition on bodily contact between monks and female nurses would create difficulties in Kelantan hospitals whereas in Thailand monks are admitted to special sections. In 1983, when the abbot of Bān Klāng needed medical treatment, he chose to be admitted to a Narathiwat hospital instead.

5. Based on figures provided by Terwiel (1979, p. 98), the average number of monks per temple in Thailand was 7.5 in 1975, while in Kelantan it was around 5.5; the highest average for Kelantan is 7.1, but this figure

is exceptional. The Deputy Chief Abbot of Kelantan conducts an annual count of monks and novices during Lent (*phansā*) but keeps no record of monks who are ordained or who leave immediately after the *phansā* period. Hence, the figures given may not be accurate since many of those ordained for a short period before or during Lent leave immediately after the *phansā* period. Although the number of novices (*nēn*) is also included in the census, no figures are kept of the number of nuns (*māechī*).

6. By definition, a "quorum" of monks (*song*), which technically makes up the *sangha*, is a grouping of four monks or more depending on the kind of ritual to be conducted (Wells 1975, p. 142; O'Connor 1978, p. 76). Thus, usually four monks are required for most rituals, but for ordination into the monkhood (*upasampada*) a minimum of five monks is the pre-requisite (Keyes 1977, p. 80; Rahula 1966, p. 154; Tambiah 1970, p. 106; Terwiel 1979, p. 210). Terwiel (1979, p. 201) mentions that four is also the minimum number of monks required to make a valid decision in the name of the *sangha*, to chant the full version of the *Patimokkha*, to expel a monk from the *sangha*, or to receive the *kathin* robes. Kaufman (1960, p. 135) mentions that "a quorum of five monks is needed to practise Buddhist law within the *bod* and to punish, make decisions and conduct most of the services". Temples with four monks or fewer must borrow monks on these occasions to make up the "quorum".

7. For instance, during a dedicatory celebration of the temple's archway (see Chapter 7), a Siamese man of Bān Klāng was ordained for three days together with two Chinese men from outside the village. It was exceptional for a Siamese to be ordained for only three days. However, this person was slightly different from most other Siamese, for he was given to heavy drinking most of the time. It was on the persistent request of his mother that he decided to "take a break" and be ordained. Since he was not really interested in doing so, he was ill-prepared for the ceremony, and had to repeat word-by-word his lines from the ordaining monks, as did the other two Chinese candidates. This case of three-day ordination for this particular man is by no means typical of the Siamese although common among the Chinese.

8. A similar pattern of behaviour is also evident in Thailand. De Young (1966, p. 116) observes that there are varying lengths of stay as monks, since not everyone aspires to be in the *sangha* for life except for a handful who eventually become abbots and temple instructors. Yet even the abbots may leave the *sangha* for a more rewarding profession, or for

other personal reasons. In Kelantan, for instance, it was rumoured that involvement with a woman, whom he later married, was the main reason for the voluntary disrobing of an abbot of a temple in Kota Bharu district. He was one of the most promising monks in the state; the residents of his village had high expectations that he would continue with the work of his predecessor, a widely known and very learned monk, who was also his maternal uncle. Alas, his love for the woman was too strong. It was even rumoured that the woman had resorted to magic to lure him away from the monkhood.

9. For instance, when a former monk needs to find employment, he can always take advantage of the contacts he had previously established while he was a monk. If he opens a business, his previous relationships with the Chinese urban community should help him tremendously. Even if he does none of these, he can at least expect to be warmly received whenever he goes to town by the Chinese patrons of the temple where he once served as a monk.

10. One cannot help but notice this, in particular when a chapter of monks are chanting. The junior monks, even after having been ordained for one year or so, seem to "slack behind" in the uttering of the chant, resorting to the old trick of coughing and clearing the throat at the instant the lines elude their memory.

11. The counting of the duration of an ordained period needs some explanation here. While the duration of a "token ordination" is given by the number of days actually spent as a monk, the longer-period type of ordination is determined by the total number of Lent (*phansā*) periods that the monk has passed through. For example, if one's stay includes the entire Lent, then one can rightfully claim to have been ordained for one Lent (that is, one *phansā*), even if the stay is shorter than one year. Another person may spend a period of more than one year but if he quits just before the beginning of the second Lent, then technically the ordained period is still considered one Lent. Hence, a monk with one *phansā* to his credit may have stayed in the temple either for much less than a whole year or for almost two years.

Chapter 4
Wat Klāng: A Village Temple

There are two temples in Bān Klāng, located in different parts of the village. Of the two only one is really central to the village's social and religious life since most rituals and ceremonies are held there rather than at the other temple. In strictly technical terms the latter, which does not have an ordination hall (*bōt; ubōsatha,* hall), is not a *wat* but a "monastic residence" (*samnaksong;* or *samnaksangha*).[1] None of the monks reside in this temple, except for one who keeps a living quarters there. However, like other monks, he spends most of his time at the first temple, where he also takes his meals since no food is sent by the villagers to the second one. Nevertheless, the second temple is not totally abandoned. On every Buddhist Sabbath (*wan phra*) monks from the first temple also come to conduct the rites here, in addition to what is going on at the main temple. This usually involves four to five elderly persons whose houses are closer to the second temple than the main one. During festive seasons, when sleeping and resting places for visitors are urgently needed, the buildings in the second temple, which remain in good repair, fulfil the need. On such occasions it is common in Kelantan for unoccupied living quarters and even the main preaching halls of temples to be converted into temporary dormitories.

The main temple of the village, called Wat Klāng in the study, is located within a well-defined area of about 1.65 hectares. The temple buildings and its grounds are located not in the middle of the village but in its eastern quarter, away from the most densely populated part of the settlement, the choice of the site perhaps in keeping with the tradition of separating monastic residents from the lay community.

Hence the temple ground looks deserted during most times of the year, except when functions are going on inside.

In its traditional layout the space within a temple compound is clearly defined into two separate areas, namely, the *buddhavāsa*, the place of worship of the Buddha by both monks and laymen; and the *sanghavāsa*, places specifically designed for the exclusive use of monks, for example, living quarters and the ordination hall (cf. Swearer 1976*a*, p. 26). However, the layout of buildings within the Bān Klāng temple grounds does not clearly reflect this type of spatial designation. Most of its buildings are located around the central feature of the *sanghavāsa*, the ordination hall (*bōt* or *ubōsatha*, hall), which is the most sacred of all temple buildings. There are also four living quarters of the monks, called *kuti*, within the same compound.

The ordination hall (structure no. 1 in Figure 4.1) orients east-west, with its main entrance facing west. In front there is a sandy yard where outdoor ceremonies take place. Whenever there is to be any procession, including the one around the hall, it becomes the mar-shalling place for the congregation. Evening sermons to commem-orate Buddhist holy days (such as *mākha*, *wisākha*, and *songkrān*) are normally delivered here. It is also the spot where dedicatory sand *cetiya*[2] are moulded during the Siamese new year and other festivals.

Within the realm of the *buddhavāsa* (where monks and the laity meet in Buddhist rituals) the most important building is the sermon hall (*māe wat*; literally, "mother temple"; Malay: *ibu ketik*). Most rituals that involve both monks and the laity are conducted in this building. The sermon hall is known by various names, but its main function is to serve as the gathering place for the large number of people attending temple functions. Religious sermons, particularly those on Buddha's teachings and code of laws (*dhamma*) are also delivered in this building; hence, it is often called "*dhamma* hall" (*rōng tham*) while some literature on Thai Buddhism refers to this building as the *vihāra*.

In religious terms the sermon hall is less sacred than the or-dination hall, but it is a building most frequently used within the temple complex. With the exception of ordination ceremonies, practically all temple business, sacred or otherwise, is conducted here including the rituals to mark the beginning and end of the Lent period (*phansā*), gift-giving ceremonies (*kathin* and *thāut phā pā*), the offering of food to the monks (*sajbāt*), and merit-making of various

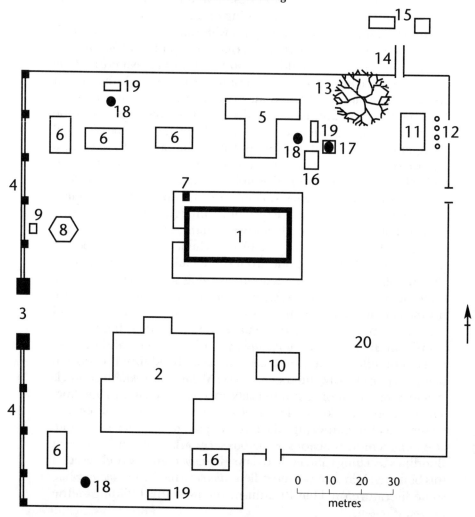

FIGURE 4.1
Plan of Wat Klāng

1. Ordination hall
2. Sermon hall
3. Archway and main entrance
4. Temple fence
5. Kitchen and dining house
6. Monks' living quarters
7. Bell tower
8. Pavilion
9. Shelter for ceremonial bathing of the abbot on his birthday
10. Structure housing the "Footprint of the Buddha" relic
11. Depositories of cremation remains
12. Miniature *cēdī* for cremation remains
13. *Bō* tree
14. Bridge leading to cremation facilities
15. Cremation facilities
16. Storage sheds
17. Water tank
18. Wells
19. Bathrooms and toilets
20. Coconut grove

kinds. Impromptu meetings of the temple lay committee are also conducted in the sermon hall. During the Lent retreat (*phansā*) nightly sermons by monks are delivered here.

Visitors are entertained in this building, where sleeping accommodation is also provided if they decide to spend the night at the temple. Living quarters of the abbot is located in this building, part of which is sectioned off for the purpose. The sermon hall also houses two altars for Buddha images (*thī phra*); both are constantly bedecked with offerings, such as incense sticks, candles, and flowers made of plastic as well as fresh ones. On one of the altars sits a life-size image of the abbot next to, but at a lower level than, a small image of the Buddha. Upon entering the sermon hall the laity usually go to this altar first in order to pay respect to the Buddha image (*wāj phra*). Only after they have done so do they turn their attention to the monks — if there are any in the hall at that time — to pay the customary respect.

The sermon hall of Wat Klāng is a large wooden structure of two storeys standing on piles. Its size is quite impressive by rural standards, with extensions sprawling from what was initially a small brick building. The first floor provides ample seating for at least 200 people, and divides into various levels to reflect the hierarchy of the Buddha images, monks, and laymen. The second storey serves only as a storeroom for kitchen utensils (large basins, huge cooking pots, serving plates, and glasses which are used during major temple functions) and pieces of timber salvaged from demolished, older temple buildings.

Behind the sermon hall is an open shed in which weekly classes in the Siamese vernacular are conducted by one of the monks.[3] These are held on Saturdays, the school weekend. Next to the school shed is a small building that houses a replica of the Buddha's footprint relic (*phraphutthabāt camlāung*), which is actually a copy made from another one found in Thailand. Other important buildings include various structures that are located across the sandy yard from the sermon hall. One of them is the kitchen house where food is usually prepared on a large scale during temple festivals; it also provides dining facilities for a large number of people. Not far from the kitchen is a building where ashes from mortuary cremations are kept in structures resembling the *cetiya*. These are called *bua*.[4] The crematorium facilities (*choeng takōn*) are located outside the temple compound across an old dried-up river bed. A concrete walkway joins the crematorium to the temple compound.

FIGURE 4.2
Floor Plan of the Sermon Hall

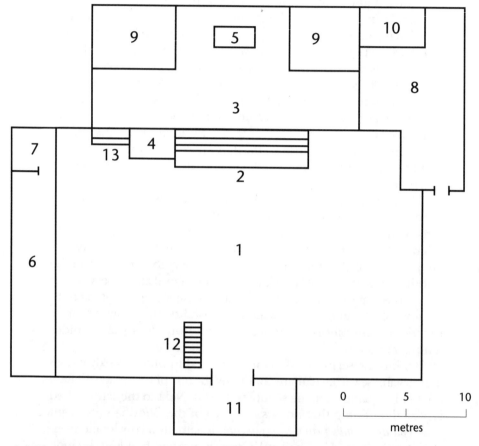

1. Main gathering area of the lay congregation
2. Stepped area where gift items are displayed
3. Raised area where monks sit during rituals
4. Altar for life-size image of the abbot
5. Altar for a small image of the Buddha
6. Raised area where monks sit at other times when talking to the laity
7. Sleeping quarters of the abbot
8. Food preparation area
9. Storerooms
10. Bathroom and toilet
11. Covered porch of the main entrance to the hall
12. Staircase leading to the upper storey of the hall
13. Steps leading to area 3

There is a *bō* tree (*ficus religiosa*) near the building that houses the *bua* structures. The present tree is said to be the "descendant" of an older one that used to grow not far away from it. Members of the congregation conduct a special rite of pouring water (*rodnām*) onto the base of the tree and also at the site of its "predecessor" during the celebration to mark the Siamese new year (*songkrān*). Hence, the new year celebration is also known locally as *chalāung tonphō* (literally, "dedicatory celebration of the *bō* tree").

In 1982 the temple population consisted of six monks including the abbot (all of them Siamese), one *phāutā*, and two *māechī*.[5] The abbot is seventy-seven years old and has been ordained for fifty-five years. He was born in Bān Klāng and is the most senior monk in the state after the Chief Monk of Kelantan. Poor health has now confined him to his living quarters for most of the time. In 1983, when his illness became very serious and required specialized treatment, he was admitted into a hospital in Narathiwat.

The abbot of Bān Klāng is a monk noted for his simplicity. While many other abbots are preoccupied with the building of enormous sermon halls, large kitchen buildings, and various structures of prestige, he appears not to be bothered by all this, for he is quite content with the buildings still standing in the compound, no matter how dated they look. The sermon hall in Bān Klāng is a pre-war timber structure, of which kind only a few still remain in Kelantan. This is in stark contrast with those of most other temples, which have brand-new brick buildings serving as sermon halls. The only newly built structure of Bān Klāng temple is an archway (*sumpratū*) erected at the main entrance to the temple grounds. This structure was built, after persistent requests by various people, with money contributed mainly by the shareholders of one of the two tobacco companies of the village.

The abbot's preference for a simple life-style appears very difficult for younger monks and for most of the villagers to comprehend. One example of this concerns the use of television sets. While television sets and a growing number of video-cassette recorders are becoming prestigious material possessions of some wealthier temples, the abbot is known to cherish no such interest. He has never openly stated his dislike for television, but expresses his view rather tacitly, as the following account well illustrates. A Chinese businessman from Kota Bharu, a dealer in electrical goods, for some unknown reason was suddenly quite anxious to donate a colour television set to the temple, an offer the abbot could not refuse since declining the offer was tantamount to an insult. Nevertheless, the abbot resorted to an elegant diplomatic manœuvre by asking the businessman to seek the consent of other monks first; should they agree, so would he. Though they admittedly would have liked to have the set, the younger monks, sensing something amiss, considered the issue at length and eventually decided to decline the offer out of respect for the abbot.

The deputy abbot is about thirty-two years old, and has served in the *sangha* for six years. Like the abbot, he was born in Bān Klāng. Before his ordination he had worked for a Chinese businessman in Kota Bharu. During this time he managed to acquire some proficiency in the Kelantanese version of Hokkien, a dialect widely spoken among the Chinese in the state. His knowledge of the dialect undoubtedly makes him indispensable in dealing with the Chinese members of the congregation. The other four monks are much younger than the deputy abbot; all are outsiders of Bān Klāng — two from Tumpat, one from Aril, and one from Kota Bharu.

The *phāutā* and one of the two *māechī* are Chinese, and both originate from Chinese settlements outside Bān Klāng. The other *māechī* is a Siamese resident of Bān Klāng. The three, all above sixty years of age, may be considered an integral part of the temple population. Although there is no formal institution for *māechī* in Kelantan, the two plus the *phāutā* are given due recognition by supporters of the temple, in particular during major temple functions. For instance, during *thāut kathin* and other merit-making ceremonies, the three monastic residents also receive their share of the ritual gifts.

The *māechī* and the *phāutā* are valuable to the monks in the sense that they minister to their needs. It is not that help from other members of the laity is not forthcoming, but rather that as full-time residents of the temple, they are better able to extend a helping hand to the monks, especially the ailing abbot, around the clock. They proved a great asset when the abbot was confined to bed in 1983 after a stroke paralysed him from the waist downwards. The three nursed the abbot, prepared his medication, saw to his special dietary requirements, and bathed him. When the abbot was hospitalized in Narathiwat, the three took turns to attend to him in the ward.

Apart from the monks and the three robed laypersons, another lay resident of the temple deserves a mention here: a slightly retarded eighteen-year-old Chinese boy who is entrusted to the care of the abbot. This appears to be quite a common practice in Kelantan. People are known to send their children or relatives under their responsibility, particularly those who are mentally retarded, to spend their time in temples. Unless they are dangerously violent, placing them under the care of the monks is a better option than having them admitted to government mental institutions. On most occasions the person is symbolically adopted by the monk. In this way the temple also provides the badly needed facilities to take in and care for the underprivileged or delinquent youngsters.[6]

To provide the monks with a daily ration of cooked food, villagers take turns to make deliveries to the main temple. Although in Thailand it is quite common for monks to go from house to house on their morning rounds to collect alms food (*pajbinthabāt*), no monks in Bān Klāng do this, except symbolically on certain days of the year.[7] Nor do monks elsewhere in Kelantan go out any longer in the morning on alms rounds. Instead, households have the food sent to the temple on a roster basis.

Sending of food to the temple helps alleviate two major problems concerning the work schedules and religious obligations of the laity: more immediately, people can now leave early for work without having to wait around for the monks to come by first. Further, if all households were to contribute food every day, the amount collected would be excessive; too much for the temple residents alone to consume, even if each household gives only a little. Waste aside, it would be too cumbersome and not worth the effort for individual households to get up very early to do the cooking, knowing full well that only a small portion of it will end up as alms. The setting up of a roster has therefore become the practice in most Siamese villages in Kelantan. The cooked food that is sent to the temple is always freshly prepared in the morning of the day it is delivered, and never left over from the previous night's meals.[8]

The roster system is also practised in some parts of Thailand. De Young notes that in northern Thailand, a village is divided into sections of between sixteen and twenty households under an appointed head, preferably one who has been previously ordained as a monk or novice (De Young 1966, p. 115). Each section is responsible for sending food to the temple. Interestingly, a bamboo bell is passed from one sector to another, and at dusk, the head of the sector who receives the bell sounds it to signal to the households under his charge that food should be sent to the temple the next morning. Usually the temple receives enough food to cover the morning and afternoon meals of its residents.

In the village studied by De Young the practice is known as "*hua muad song kow*" (literally, "head section send rice") and appears to be a strictly northern Thai innovation (De Young 1966, p. 116). Kershaw (1981, p. 93) says that in the village he studied the roster system is known as *nirān*. Although he does not elaborate on the origin of the term, I suggest it may have derived from *nirāndōn*, meaning "perpetuity", a term which signifies the never-ending cycle of the roster. I have not heard the term *nirān* used in Bān Klāng, but *jok khāw* and *jok āhān*, meaning "taking rice, taking food (to the temple)", are used instead.

In Bān Klāng, on a normal day two households prepare food for the temple. The household members concerned, always the women-folk, make sure that they have no other commitments for the day since they also have to wait and serve the food to the monks. There are two occasions for this, one in the morning and another just before noon. If the roster runs smoothly, there is usually a lapse (*wen*) of about thirty days before it is the same household's turn again to prepare food for the monks. At most, therefore, a household needs to prepare food for the temple only once every month. However, not every household is included in the roster. Exemptions apply to house-holds consisting of single males, or of couples who are too old even to cook for themselves and who eat from their children's kitchens of a separate household.

The roster is faithfully followed by all the households involved except in emergencies, in which case arrangements are made with other households for relief of duty or for the turn to be passed on to the next household. It is considered a serious breach of com-munity norms for a household to miss its turn out of forgetfulness, or to knowingly miss it for whatever reasons without having first made arrangements for relief.[9] The roster is not exclusive either; that is, any household may also send food to the temple on any day at all, even on days that are not its turn to do so. This applies to food known to be the favourite of some particular monks and to delicacies which cannot be kept until the household's turn comes along. For instance, those who have just returned from a trip abroad may bring back specially prepared food and various kind of treats; to prevent spoilage these are given immediately, irrespective of the donors' turn in the roster.[10] Exotic food purchased from across the border in Thailand is often presented to the monks on the day it reaches the village, provided it arrives before noon. Otherwise, it is kept overnight and given to the monks first thing the following morning.

As mentioned above, the roster ensures a continuous supply of cooked food for temple residents. However, food is just one aspect of temple life. Money is also needed to finance the running of temple affairs with a comfortable degree of prosperity and grandeur, while monks, despite the austerity of the lives they lead, need money for various purposes, such as to buy items for personal use and to pay for their transport costs. The temple also has to maintain and repair its buildings and to pay for various running expenses, such as electricity bills as well as items for the use of its residents: mainly household goods such as mats, mattresses, mosquito nets, floor coverings, electric ceiling fans, water pumps, cooking utensils, and kitchen equipment. Some items for ritual use such as candles, incense sticks, and matches have to be bought by the temple itself, using its own funds, to supplement those donated by the general public. Even though the temple receives a daily contribution of cooked food, it also has to buy and keep as a contingency measure an additional supply of other kinds of food, in particular boxes of soft drinks, canned milk, sugar, coffee, tea, biscuits, tobacco, betel leaves, areca nuts, and cigarettes, some of which are eventually served to visitors.

The Lay Community That
Supports the Temple: Phuak Wat

A temple usually relies for material support on the residents of the village in which it is located, as well as on people of villages far afield and from the urban and rural Chinese communities. The lay community which supports the temple, by way of making merit there in preference to other temples and through attending and sponsoring most of the temple's rituals and ceremonies, is termed *phuak wat* (Bunnag 1973, p. 65). Since the group may include anybody at all who patronizes the temple in any way whatsoever, its nature is all-encompassing and the concept is therefore quite loose in its actual operation.

In general, *phuak wat* consists of two types of people. The first are those who live in the village where the temple is located; by tradition they are automatically *phuak wat* members of that particular temple. The second category consists of village outsiders; they are usually rural Chinese of various settlements in Kelantan, town-based *peranakan* Chinese, and Siamese of villages without temples. In many cases there is an overlap of membership: some people who are already *phuak wat* members of one temple often support other temples simultaneously, in particular when the resident monks happen to be their relatives. Very often one finds that a *phuak wat* member of one temple may also be sponsoring ceremonies in temples at other places; this is to be expected, given the overlapping nature of the *phuak wat* membership.

The main thing about *phuak wat* of the second category is that the size of their membership depends on a temple's popularity and its ability to appeal to a large number of people. Therefore, to be popular a temple normally has often to orient itself beyond functions which are purely religious in nature. Some temples are known to have resident monks who are skilled practitioners of traditional medicine. Such temples become a focus for visitors, especially during the weekends and public holidays. Senior monks whom the laity believe possess supernatural power (*saksīt*) often attract an even larger number of visitors to their temples, not only from the immediate neighbourhood but also from places as far away as Singapore and Kuala Lumpur.

All sorts of services are solicited by these visitors. While some may come out of curiosity to meet a monk of repute, others seek the monk's blessing so that their business ventures may prosper and their children pass their coming school examinations brilliantly. Some may ask for magical objects, such as talismans and pieces of cloth written with sacred formulae, to be used for a variety of purposes, for instance, to protect oneself against danger, to make oneself attractive in a courtship one is about to embark upon, and to be successful at job interviews. Some even come to obtain winning numbers in four-digit lotteries. The request can also be very personal and most intimate; in one case the help of a well-known monk was sought by the wife of a Singaporean Chinese civil servant who, anxious to see that her husband got an overdue promotion, insisted that the monk use his magical influence so that the official's immediate superior would be more sympathetic. Another Chinese, also from Singapore, was about to go through a court case; he asked the same monk to dispense a magical formula so that the judge's decision could be influenced in his favour.[11] With such kinds of services, many temples tend to have a large number of visitors whose contributions to the monastic income can be quite considerable.

As for the temple in Bān Klāng, its *phuak wat* theoretically consists of everyone staying in the village and of people originally from Bān Klāng who now live elsewhere. The latter consider Bān Klāng as their ancestral home to which they return regularly for whatever reason, including attendance at the temple functions. This group includes those who have migrated temporarily to towns to work and people who are now living in the *nikhom* land settlement projects in Thailand. Despite being permanently established in the *nikhom*, many recognize their kinship ties with Bān Klāng. They consider it their ancestral village and accordingly prefer to make merit at its temple rather than elsewhere.

Apart from that, *phuak wat* members of Bān Klāng's temple also include people whom I call, for want of a better term, "freelance" supporters. Complete outsiders, they support the temple in Bān Klāng for various reasons. Although they do not consider themselves members of Bān Klāng's residential community, they are nevertheless members of the temple's congregation. In many cases they also visit a series of temples on their rounds, mainly during weekends, and because of this I call them "weekend pilgrims". An interesting thing about this group of people is that they may have come from villages that already have temples of their own. "Weekend pilgrims" and "freelance" supporters of Bān Klāng include Chinese of various rural settlements and towns, among them Kota Bharu, Kuala Krai, Pasir Puteh, Tanah Merah, and Machang. Siamese of villages that have no temples of their own are also included in this collectivity of supporters. During weekends the temple becomes the converging point for village outsiders and Chinese members of the *phuak wat*.

As mentioned, some of the Chinese supporters have kinship ties not only with Chinese residents of Bān Klāng but also with some Siamese of the village as a result of intermarriages between earlier Chinese migrants and Siamese women. The exact nature of their present kinship relatedness is quite difficult to establish since mixed marriages between Siamese and Chinese do not now take place as

often as it did in the past. However, a large number of Siamese and
Chinese acknowledge that they have between them some kind of
ancestral kinship ties by virtue of earlier mixed marriages. Some
town-dwelling Chinese could therefore claim strong justification for
patronizing Bān Klāng's temple. By invoking genealogical connections with the Siamese, they proclaim the village to be the home of
their forbears.

By its very nature, the membership of a *phuak wat* is large since it
includes people from various villages and towns. Because of the way
the *phuak wat* of one temple overlaps with those of other temples and
because it also includes "freelance" supporters and "weekend pilgrims," Bān Klāng's *phuak wat* at first appears to be loosely organized.
However, central to the *phuak wat* is a select group of laymen called
sangkhārī. This consists of those who play special roles in organizing
temple affairs and who oversee and control the day-to-day running
of the temple. The *sangkhārī* are *bona fide* residents of Bān Klāng;
they were born in the village and had served as monks for a considerable number of years. In Bān Klāng the *sangkhārī* is a committee
of five people, four of them Siamese and one Chinese. The Siamese
committee members are ex-monks of four to six years' standing in
the *sangha*. The Chinese *sangkhārī* member, in contrast, was ordained
for only one year. Notwithstanding his short stay as a monk, his
position on the committee somehow possesses a certain prominence
simply because he is the father of Bān Klāng's headman.[12]

Members of the *sangkhārī* group combine the roles of ritual
leaders, treasurers, caretakers of temple properties, and public-
relations officers. During temple rituals they lead the congregation
as *phūnam*.[13] Because of their close association with the monks, they
are also in a better position to advise others on details concerning
ritual procedures. For instance, when the laity want to make an
offering of goods to the monks, they will first seek the *sangkhārī's*
advice. Since monks, in respect of rules governing monastic
discipline, are not supposed to express openly their desire for any
particular gift,[14] any knowledgeable person will have to consult the
sangkhārī members on the matter.

The *sangkhārī* members also keep an inventory of temple properties. When co-ordinating gifts from various potential donors,
they ensure that the temple is neither short of, nor oversupplied
with, specific kinds of items. Acting as temple spokesmen, the

sangkhārī members are responsible for informing the public of forthcoming ceremonies and other religious events.

In the religious ranking among unrobed persons, *sangkhārī* members enjoy an elevated status, higher than other supporters of the temple. Lester mentions that in Southeast Asian Theravāda Buddhist society, there are two categories of laymen — the ordained and the unordained adult males who are former monks may enjoy a distinctly higher status and play a more prominent role than the rest of the laity, and can consequently become lay ritual leaders on the Buddhist Sabbath (*wan phra*) and in a number of rituals which do not require the presence of a monk (Lester 1973, p. 131).

In Bān Klāng one of the *sangkhārī* members has been ordained for six years and spent most of that time in Thailand. He is one of the few ex-monks in Kelantan with sufficient experience in the *sangha* for him to enjoy the title of *ācān wat*, an honour reserved for those qualified to give instruction and teach monastic rules to newly ordained monks. His many years of performing such duties have given rise to the clear impression that, on occasions, he may be more knowledgeable than any of the monks or other villagers in discussions of the finer points of temple rituals. The abbot is perhaps an exception, but nevertheless he does consult him on some occasions. Because of his superb knowledge of temple procedures and the Buddhist religion, the *ācān wat* is accorded a prominent position in the status hierarchy of the village, perhaps just below that of the monks.

An *ācān wat* is not necessarily a person who has been a monk longest; what is important is the kind of authority that he embodies. Therefore, it is normal to expect him to lead the lay congregation during rituals. At temple functions he executes this role with an air of confidence and authority, and people always look to him for guidance and advice on ritual and religious matters. This is in accord with Terwiel's observation in Thailand: at most rituals the lay leadership usually falls on a person who is superior to all others present in terms of religious knowledge and age (Terwiel 1979, p. 195).

Despite the position of respect he commands, the *ācān wat* of Bān Klāng leads a spartan existence, owning nothing more than the bare essential household goods, except for a television set and a radio, which to him are necessary to keep abreast with the latest developments in Thailand. To him Thailand represents everything ideal as a place to lead a true Buddhist religious and social life. He also owns some land, which he rents out to others for tobacco planting. Although the rent is barely adequate to support him, his income is supplemented by gifts of money and goods (mainly food and some articles of clothing) from people who come to consult him from time to time. Apart from being a *sangkhārī* member, he is also a specialist in traditional medicine (*māu*; Malay: *bomoh*); his other speciality is Thai astrology. Other than residents of Bān Klāng, his large clientele includes both Malay and Chinese outsiders.[15] During weekends, it is quite common for the Chinese to come for consultations with the *ācān wat* on matters ranging from fortune-telling to giving advice on the most auspicious day to travel or to start a business.

The leading roles played by the *sangkhārī* members, particularly by the *ācān wat*, are comparable to those of the person whom Swearer calls the "layman *extraordinaire*" (Swearer 1976*b*). In parts of northern Thailand, this particular personality becomes the intermediary between the *sangha* and the laity during rituals, and because of the expert knowledge that these personalities have gained while in the monkhood, laymen *extraordinaires* are also addressed by the respectful title of *phāu khrū*. Acting as the masters of ceremony, they are consulted by the laity for proper guidance not only in merit-making acts but also in other areas of ritual activity from which monks are excluded, either because of monastic regulations or because of "the symbolic limits inherent in the monk's role" (ibid., p. 158).

Apart from the lay congregation (*phuak wat*) which supports the temple and the lay steering committee (*sangkhārī*), there is another group of people whose function and membership varies from time to time. This group I term the temple's *ad hoc* committee. When the temple wants to organize an extraordinary function, for instance, a dedicatory celebration (*ngān chalāung*) to mark the completion of a building project, this committee is quickly formed. Members of this committee divide between themselves the responsibilities of organizing the event. This committee, called *kammakan wat*, comprises a number of men (never women) who occupy prestigious positions in the community: resident monks of the village, the headman, elderly members of the community, and also several distinguished outsiders. The last includes especially prominent Chinese businessmen and community leaders, as well as distinguished monks of various temples in Kelantan and Thailand.

The inclusion of outsiders in the *kammakan wat* is quite logical, indeed pragmatic. Some of the well-known Chinese businessmen and community leaders have good contacts with the wider Chinese population in Kelantan on whose support the Siamese are dependent for material and monetary donations. Apart from that they also have good contacts with the Malay leadership and bureaucrats. Excellent rapport with Malay government officers helps to facilitate dealings with the local authority. For instance, an application for a permit to hold a shadow-puppet show at the temple tends to be issued with a minimum of fuss if it is arranged through those who are on friendly terms with officials at the district office. Hence, Chinese businessmen or community leaders who are known to be very smooth in dealing with Malay officials are included in the working committee of the temple for pragmatic reasons.

This is typical of the brokerage role played by the Chinese community in Kelantan for the Siamese. Politically active Chinese are known to mediate on behalf of the Siamese in order to secure government aid for temples (Kershaw 1973, p. 3). This brokerage is not limited to temple functions alone. Even arrangements to have electricity installed in the village are often facilitated by these intermediaries. To cite another example, during the function held in May 1983 to celebrate the completion of the temple's archway a troop of dancers and musicians was brought over from Thailand by the organizing committee. The special permit required for this was obtained with a minimum of difficulty from the local authority, thanks to the mediation of an influential Chinese supporter of the temple.

The number of people who are appointed to the *kammakan wat* membership varies according to the requirements of the situation: large-scale temple functions call for more people to be involved in their organization, but for smaller functions, fewer people sit on the committee. The inclusion in the working committee of well-known monks of other temples definitely adds prestige and glamour to the event, thus attracting more people to the function.

So far it has been shown that the temple of Bān Klāng is central to village identity. Nearly all households provide support and sustenance to the temple, at least through the roster system mentioned above. Irrespective of ethnicity, nearly all households are involved in this daily routine. Participation in activities centred on the temple draws Bān Klāng residents together into a single and integrated community. Without the temple, Bān Klāng would hardly be a rural settlement, only a conglomeration of houses and tobacco-farmers lacking common bond and interest.

However, closer examination reveals that the organization of temple affairs is controlled by permanent members of the clergy and the religious élite of the village, the membership of both these groups being almost exclusively Siamese. Despite the fact that more than half of the village population is Chinese, no Chinese residents of Bān Klāng have chosen the monkhood as a lifelong vocation. The best that the Chinese can do in terms of a sustained period of monastic membership is exemplified by the *māechī* and the *phāutā*, but their role is neither decisive nor indispensable in the running of temple affairs. In fact, compared with these two categories of robed personnel, other laymen are more influential in matters concerning temple organization, and these *sangkhārī* are Siamese, with the exception of one Chinese. As the case of Bān Klāng demonstrates, even in a village with a sizeable Chinese population, the staffing of the temple and the membership of the religious élite are almost exclusively Siamese. The Chinese nevertheless participate in the rituals held at the temple; and by doing so they are able to proclaim themselves members of the same community as the Siamese.

The involvement of the Chinese in temple affairs is limited, however, to the extent that they have only restricted access to the body of Buddhist religious knowledge. Despite their participation in and sponsorship of temple events, the Chinese remain essentially "outsiders" to the gamut of rituals and ceremonies associated with Theravāda Buddhism. Yet to the Siamese, the temple means more that just a place of worship. In it lie the cultural resources upon which the Siamese draw to support their claim to a distinct ethnic identity in a way that is not possible for the Chinese, their co-religionist and co-resident of the same village. Siamese persistence in maintaining various temple traditions has its underlying cultural reasons; it serves to articulate Siamese cultural identity.

NOTES

1. On this distinction see, for instance, Wells (1975, p. 27). I was told by infomants that in Thailand, if a *samnaksong* is not lived in for a certain

number of years, the land on which it stands will revert to the government. However, as soon as a place has been consecrated as a *wat*, that is, whenever an ordination building (*bōt*) has been constructed, the land on which it stands will be perpetually granted to the *sangha*, even if the *wat* were to be abandoned at some later stage. In Kelantan, an abandoned *samnaksong* or *wat* never faces this problem since no law regarding this exists. Legally, temple land in Kelantan is classified as similar in status to burial grounds or other kinds of land set aside for religious purposes, such as for mosques. Such lands, classified as *tanah wakaf*, are exempt from taxes.

2. These forms are made of sand brought from outside the temple's compound and shaped like *cetiya*. They are often decorated with flags and flowers. Traditionally, the main objective of building the *cetiya* is to bring in as much sand as possible so that over the years the temple compound will become higher than the level of surrounding areas, making it less susceptible to muddiness during rainy seasons. The building of the *cetiya* in general has great religious significance (see Swearer 1976a, p. 53). Although the compound of Wat Klāng is already on high ground, sand *cetiya* are still made as part of temple tradition.

3. In October 1983 this shed was pulled down to make way for a community hall (Malay: *balai raya*), the construction of which was fully funded by the government. Presumably, Siamese language classes are now conducted in this new building.

4. These structures are called *bua* although in standard Thai this term means the lotus flower. But the shape of the structure itself resembles the lotus bud.

5. The *phāutā* and *māechī* are, respectively, male and female ascetics who observe the ten precepts and lead a reclusive life within the temple. They dress themselves in white garments which in Buddhist terms are the insignia of a pious layperson (Tambiah 1984, p. 386, fn. 13). The women are not actually *bhikkhuni* in the traditional sense. The men are neither novices nor fully ordained monks. In terms of status, a *māechī* is considered to be at the lowest level of those in robes in the *wat* hierarchy (Kaufman 1960, p. 121), but they and the *phāutā* exemplify the closest a layperson can approach asceticism without actually being ordained. For further details on the institution of the *māechī*, see Cook (1981) and Keyes (1984, p. 229). For a further elaboration of the *phāutā*, see Tambiah (1984, pp. 296, 386).

6. Bān Klāng's temple is not the only one providing this charitable service. In 1982 the temple in Bangsae also accommodated a Chinese recluse

from Pulau Pinang. He is not exactly insane, but he shows some kind of psychotic tendencies. Golomb (1978, p. 88) observes that in the Siamese village he studied there were two psychotic Chinese "patients" whose fees were paid by their relatives. In Bān Klāng no fees are paid, but the parents of the Chinese boy do send money, clothing, and food regularly for his upkeep. See also Kaufman (1960, p. 115) for a discussion on similar temple functions in Thailand.

7. Particularly on the day preceding the Lent period, that is, on *wan āsālahabūchā*, on the first two days of Lent, and also on the last day of the Lent retreat. For details on this, see Chapter 5.

8. One might ask here why one should not give the monks food left over from the previous night, or for that matter why should one not cook a little extra to give the monks the next day. To do either of these would defeat the purpose of giving. Since the giving of food to monks symbolizes the utmost in the laity's support of the monks and the *sangha*, a gift of leftover food nullifies the merit that would otherwise be gained. In fact, according to informants, the preparation of food to be given to monks involves strict observance of procedures to ensure that, even by default the food so prepared will not be considered as a "leftover". For example, food is technically regarded as a "leftover" if it is merely tasted (*chim dū*), say to see whether the correct amount of salt or sugar has been added, while it is being cooked. By tasting the cook actually "touches" the food, rendering the remainder a "leftover", and so not worthy of being offered to monks.

9. The question of missing the roster is a hypothetical one here, for it seldom occurs. Furthermore, two households are always involved every day. Should one miss its turn, there is always the other to ensure that food is sent to the temple. Normally food sent by the two households is more than enough to feed all the temple residents. During my fieldwork, I did not come across any household that had missed its turn, nor had there been any shortage of cooked food on any particular day.

10. In Aril, I noticed that a monk who had just returned from Johor Bahru after a long stay at a temple there was feasted with his favourite food by relatives on the day he was back in the village. Not only that, but he was served the food on the veranda of his living quarters, rather than in the kitchen of the temple where other monks were also eating.

11. There are also lay magicians in most Siamese villages who specialize in the making of love potions; their clients include members of the royalty. Golomb (1978, p. 71) mentions the case of a minor wife of a king who travelled all the way from a west coast state to fetch some "love medi-

cine" from one of the specialists (*māu sanē*) to enable her to win back the affections of her estranged husband. What Golomb does not say is that the distressed lady was actually a Chinese; she was converted to Islam prior to her marriage to the king.

12. The headman himself does not sit on the committee. One of the likely reasons is that he has never been ordained himself, not even for a "token" period. As such he does not have the right experience that is usually required of a person who wants to be a member of the steering committee.

13. Swearer (1976*b*, p. 160) also calls this ritual actor *phāu khrū.*

14. On this rule, see, for instance, Nanamoli Thera, particularly with regard to the "30 Cases Entailing Expiation with Forfeiture", that is, rules 8, 9, and 10 (Nanamoli Thera 1966, pp. 36–40).

15. In 1982 I was present when a Malay woman consulted the *ācān wat* concerning her husband's marriage to a second wife. She dreaded divorce and asked for some magical charms to entice her husband back. For this she was given sacralized face powder and lip wax, together with instructions on how to use them effectively. The distressed Malay woman was by no means exceptional. There have been others who came to seek the help of the *ācān wat* for various domestic problems.

Chapter 5
Pattern of Rituals

In Thai Buddhism, most temple rituals and ceremonies centre on merit-making (*thambun*). This is a very broad concept but in the context of temple ceremonies, merit-making is closely associated with the offering of gifts (*thawāj khryangthān*), including food, to members of the *sangha.* Money also constitutes a significant part of the gifts and if offered it is likely to assume the form of the ubiquitous money-tree (*ton ngōen*), admittedly an artistic creation which incorporates, among other things, the elements of conspicuous display of wealth.[1] In fact, at times the money-trees donated, which are ostentatiously displayed for days on end, tend to overshadow the religious significance of other presentation items, particularly the yellow robes and the alms bowls, two of the most basic requisites for a monastic way of living.

Despite the special attention shown towards the money-trees, food offering seems to be always the symbol *par excellence* of the laity's support of the monkhood. The gift of food to monks, especially when they come calling on their daily rounds, is one of many ways that villagers can make merit right their door steps. On the other hand, because of the roster system mentioned earlier, the daily offering of food to the monks is now no longer a religious activity conducted daily, in which the entire village is involved. Instead, food is now sent to the temple, which means that only a limited number of people, mainly housewives, are involved, while men and the rest of the residents are likely to be left out from the exercise.

Because of this limitation imposed by practicality and because devout Buddhists experience a conscious need to re-emphasize publicly, every now and then, the utmost significance of the offering of food to monks, a special rite — a highly revered, though seemingly simple act of placing cooked rice into the monks' bowls — is always performed collectively during most temple functions. This ritual, known as *sajbāt* or *thakbāt*, forms an integral part of major temple ceremonies. While this rite is a purely symbolic act, since only a small portion of all the cooked rice eventually collected is consumed by temple residents, people still insist on doing it, even when the containers lined up to supplement the limited holding capacity of the alms bowls are already holding far beyond capacity. Evidently, a large quantity of rice is collected in this manner even though each member of the laity present serves only one or two spoonfuls. Such is the emphasis on this particular ritual act that almost no temple ritual or religious undertaking takes place without having incorporated it. Usually conducted on the last day of a temple's major function, the *sajbāt* rite is a special event in its own right, always publicized well in advance in conjunction with the main event. On most occasions it is a rite held indoors in the sermon hall, and involves nearly all of the laity who are to be found inside the building as well as those waiting anxiously outside, who moved in as soon as the rite is about to commence.

Merit-making, apart from the gift of material goods and money, and the symbolic placing of cooked rice into the alms bowls, also includes other charitable acts which support the well-being of the temple and its residents. Thus contributions towards the construction and maintenance of temple buildings or the purchase of land or parks for the use of the *sangha* are considered worthy of merit. Although land has now become too expensive a commodity to be given away to the monastic community, a number of Kelantanese temples are known to have been built on donated lands. But the laity's support for the temples through merit-making may assume other forms as well, some indirect. For instance, many temples, as mentioned in previous chapters, often undertake the construction of new buildings or the renovation of existing ones. Building materials are normally bought at Chinese stores whose owners are either benefactors of the temples or people known to the monks. Such purchases are always made at huge discounts if not at cost, the shopowners justifying this as their special way of helping the temple, and admittedly as their version of merit-making too.

As often observed by anthropologists studying Thai society,

merit-making through gift-giving is culturally more valued than merit-making through the observance of the Buddhist precepts and the pursuit of Buddhist ethical aims. The most important thing about merit-making through gift-giving ceremonies is that it occasions the mobilization of the whole village, centring the attention of its members on the temple and its monks (Tambiah 1970, p. 57). In Kelantan merit-making also provides the pretext for people, not only from the same village but also from villages far afield who otherwise would have remained isolated from one another, to be socially mobilized. It also brings together the Siamese and the Chinese under a single religious congregation.

Gift-giving to temples and monks, apart from the persuance of merit, provides the opportunity for a public show of status. The array of goods given to the temple indicates the material wealth and prestige not only of the givers, but also of the congregation and of the village supporting the temple. One must consider this point in order to account for the overt display of all gift items during such occasions. For instance, during merit-making ceremonies associated with *kathin* and *thāut phā pā*, all gift items are prominently displayed in the sermon hall, prior to their final presentation. Sponsors are quite intent on seeing that their gifts are properly assembled for all to see. Under the guidance and assistance of members of the temple steering committee (*sangkhārī*) the sponsor of the function arranges the gift items at a prominent location within the sermon hall. In Bān Klāng this particular spot is the stepped area leading to the upper level of the hall. It is the most strategic location, being the first place that strikes anybody's attention, next to the altar where an image of the Buddha and the image of the abbot are installed; the laity and monks always go to this altar to make reverence (*wāj phra*) whenever they first enter the hall. The altar and the stepped area face outwards into the spacious hall and anything that is placed there is bound to look prominent and conspicuous.[2] If only limited space is left within the area, larger items are placed on the floor immediately below. These items are paraded around the temple compound on the day of the ceremony as the grand finale of the day's event. No secret is made of the expenses involved, and the total cost is openly talked about, even within the earshot of the sponsor.

Also on display are the ever-present *ton ngōen*, the symbolic money-trees made of banknotes of various denominations, of Malaysian and

Thai currencies. The number of trees presented depends on how grand the occasion is; the bigger ceremonies see the stepped area flooded with trees of different makes and designs, often engulfing other smaller but religiously significant gift items. While money could simply be donated to the temple in ways less conspicuous, for instance, by putting it discreetly into a donation box or an alms bowl designated as a receptor for cash contributions, its presentation in the form of money-trees adds definite colour and glamour to the occasion, especially when some of them are subjected to a noisy and colourful parade around the temple ground after being displayed in the sermon hall for days. The people put great efforts into the making of these trees, using their most imaginative ideas and obviously putting in a great deal of money as well.

The Ritual Calendar

As in other Siamese settlements in Kelantan, Bān Klāng's ritual calendar is set according to lunar dates (*cantharakhati*). This has always been the practice as far as the Siamese themselves can remember. Because of the emphasis on lunar dates certain ceremonies may not necessarily coincide with those conducted in Thailand.[3] For instance, the *songkrān* festival, an annual event celebrated on 13 April in Thailand, is celebrated at an earlier date in Bān Klāng to coincide with the exact lunar calculation (that is, on the fifteenth day of the waxing moon of the fifth lunar month). In 1983 the *songkrān* festival was celebrated in Bān Klāng on 28 March, about two weeks ahead of the date it was officially celebrated in Thailand. However, Bān Klāng also celebrates 13 April although on a much smaller scale than the one held on 28 March.

The precise use of lunar reckoning also means that extra rituals have to conducted in the event of a leap year (*athikamāt*).[4] The schedule of events for a leap year, in which there are thirteen months instead of twelve, varies from that of an ordinary year. To account for this variation, a number of the ritual occasions are held twice (see Table 5.2). For instance, during an ordinary lunar year two occasions of food offering are made to the "returned spirit of the dead" (*prēt*):[5] once in the middle of the tenth lunar month (about early September) and again at the end of the month. In contrast, during a leap year an extra occasion is planned for a similar ritual, making a total of three. When asked for explanation, many villagers insist that because of the extra month in the year, the *prēt* may become confused and return to the village in the wrong month, presumably earlier than expected. To be on the safe side, the extra occasion is held in addition and prior to the two usual ones in case the confused *prēt* should return on the right day but in the wrong month.

Tables 5.1 and 5.2 list the major temple rituals conducted in the village, in an ordinary year and in a leap year, respectively. The main difference between the two tables is that in the first, all ritual occasions are held once but in the second many are held twice. Hence there are two occasions for the celebration of *mākhabūchā*, *wisākhabūchā*, and *songkrān*. There was also an additional occasion for the ritual of food offering to the *prēt*. However, not all occasions are repeated. For instance, the rituals to mark the beginning and the end of the Lent season (*phansā*) are held only once even for a leap year.

Major temple rites are determined by the lunar dates which correspond with the anniversary of major events during the life of the Buddha. Hence during the month of January, which normally coincides with the third lunar month, the most important ceremony is *mākhabūchā*, commemorating the historic and unprecedented gathering of 1,250 monks from the four corners of the earth. In Bān Klāng this is celebrated on a moderate scale, the main ceremony being at night when a procession of people bearing candles takes place followed by the reading of a special sermon outdoors. The ceremony in the morning involves the offering of food to the monks and the *sajbāt* rite.

The next calendrical rite at the temple is the celebration of the Siamese lunar new year (*songkrān*), which takes place in March. In Bān Klāng and elsewhere in Kelantan, it is celebrated on a different day from that in Thailand. It also includes a *sajbāt* rite and the offering of food to monks. The fifth lunar month is associated with elderly people, mainly of two generations removed; hence merit-making during *songkrān* is also known as "merit-making for old folks" (*thambun khon kāe*). In some places, *songkrān* is celebrated (for the second time) on the day it is held in Thailand. In Bān Klāng the second celebration of *songkrān* also takes place, although on a smaller scale than the one held earlier.

The *wisākha* celebration which commemorates the enlightenment and the death of the Buddha is held in Bān Klāng in a manner

TABLE 5.1
Major Temple Ceremonies in 1982

Date	Siamese Lunar Calendar	Events
28 March	15th day waxing moon; 5th month	*Songkrān* — this is the one celebrated in the village
13 April	2nd day waxing moon; 6th month	*Songkrān* — this is the one officially celebrated in Thailand; also celebrated on a limited scale in Bān Klāng and a few other Siamese villages
7 May	15th day waxing moon; 6th month	*Wisākha* day
4 July	14th day waxing moon; 8th month	Eve of *āsālahabūchā*
5 July	15th day waxing moon; 8th month	*Āsālahabūchā*; this day is also the birthday of the abbot
6 July	1st day waning moon; 8th month	Beginning of the Buddhist Lent; *Sajbāt*
3 September	1st day waning moon; 10th month	*Sajrān* — food offering to the *prēt*
17 September	15th day waning moon; 10th month	*Songrān* — the second and the last occasion of food offering to the *prēt*
2 October	15th day waxing moon; 11th month	End of the Lent period
8 October	6th day waning moon; 11th month	*Kathin* ceremony

quite similar to *mākhabūchā* above, with a candlelight procession at night and the delivering of a sermon in the sandy courtyard facing the ordination hall of the temple. The ritual offering of food to monks and the *sajbāt* rite takes precedent in the morning of the same day.

The next temple rites take place over the three days that mark the beginning of the Lent retreat (*phansā*) around July (eighth lunar month). The day before the first day of the retreat is known as

TABLE 5.2
Major Temple Ceremonies in 1983 (A Lunar Leap Year)

Date	Siamese Lunar Calendar	Events
28 January	15th day waxing moon; 3rd month	*Mākhabūchā* — the first of two in a lunar leap year
26 February	15th day waxing moon; 4th month	Second *mākhabūchā* for a lunar leap year (this is indicated in the Thai calendar as the official one in Thailand)
28 March	15th day waxing moon; 5th month	*Songkrān* — this is the one celebrated traditionally in Bān Klāng
13 April	2nd day waning moon; 6th month	*Songkrān* — this is the official day of celebration in Thailand, also celebrated on a small scale in Bān Klāng
26 April	15th day waxing moon; 6th month	The first *wisākha* for a lunar leap year
26 May	15th day waxing moon; 7th month	The second *wisākha* for a lunar leap year (this is the official celebration day in Thailand as indicated in the Thai calendar)
25 June	1st day waning moon; 8th month	This day has its special significance because in an ordinary year (i.e. a non-leap year) it marks the beginning of the Buddhist Lent
13 July	14th day waxing moon; second 8th month	Eve of *āsālahabūchā*
24 July	15th day waxing moon; second 8th month	*Āsālahabūchā*; also the birthday celebration of the abbot
25 July	1st day waning moon; second 8th month	Beginning of the Lent period for a lunar leap year
6 September	14th day waning moon; 9th month	*Sajrān* — the first in the series of three for a lunar leap year
22 September	1st day waning moon; 10th month	*Sajrān* — the second one for a lunar leap year
6 October	15th day waxing moon; 10th month	*Songrān* — the last in the series of three for a lunar leap year
21 October	15th day waxing moon; 11th month	End of the Lent period
28 October	7th day waning moon; 11th month	Presentation of gifts to monks and temple — *thāut kathin*

āsālahabūchā. The *āsālaha* commemorates Buddha's first discourse to his first five disciples at the Deer Park in Benares. The commemoration also entails a procession by candlelight and an outdoor sermon similar to the one held on *mākhabūchā* celebration. In Bān Klāng *āsālaha* day has a further significance in that it is also the birthday of the abbot. In the afternoon the abbot is given a ceremonial bath by some of the congregation at the temple. Hence, this occasion is also known as *wan ābnām phāu than* (literally, the day of bathing the Reverend Father).

The ceremonial bathing of the more senior abbots to celebrate their birthdays seems to be a common practice in many temples in Kelantan. Members of the temple's congregation and monks take part in pouring scented water over the person of the abbot who is seated on a specially erected dais sheltered by a canopy of white cloth about 1 metre square. Usually a temporary structure is built in the temple compound for this purpose but in Bān Klāng a more permanent one has been constructed (structure no. 9 in Figure 4.1). An interesting point about this ritual bathing is that the bath water running off the body of the abbot is thought to be auspicious. Hence many people, especially women and children, collect as much of the water as they can by holding a number of containers close to the abbot's body as scented water is being poured onto him from above the white cloth. The water is used to wash one's face, and as a base ingredient for various medicinal concoctions and magical formula; some is poured into the well at one's house so as to sacralize its content. Since the celebration is also associated with a birthday, a number of wealthy Chinese from the towns choose to donate Western-style birthday cakes, complete with candles and decorations, for the abbot to cut, apparently a trendy element adapted to the traditional temple practice.

The three days which announce the beginning of Lent are also significant in terms of a re-enactment of the traditional practice of monks going out to collect alms food (*pajbinthabāt*). In a symbolic act echoing the practice that is common in Thailand, monks enact the rite of approaching the laity to collect food. It is symbolic partly because in the case of Bān Klāng no monks actually go from house to house to do so, but the act of collecting food is performed right in the temple compound near the sermon hall and the ordination building. On the eve of *āsālaha*, on the *āsālaha* day itself, and on the first day of Lent, residents of the village and outsiders who are members of the temple's *phuak wat* stand in a line which extends from the entrance of the ordination hall to the temple gate, with containers of cooked rice ready in their hands. As the monks pass along, spoonfuls of rice are placed into their bowls. With the exception of the bed-ridden abbot, all monks of the temple take part in this symbolic act of *pajbinthabāt*.

On the first day of Lent, a merit-making rite in the form of the offering of yellow cloth and accessories takes place. Traditionally, the Lent retreat, apparently in reference to its ancient observance in India, is associated with the rainy season but in Kelantan the wet season usually starts well after July, normally from November onwards. Nevertheless, the gift-giving occasion is still known as the offering of "cloth for the rainy season" (*thawāj phā ābnāmfon*). Usually this gift-giving ceremony is privately sponsored and only family members of the sponsor are involved. The event takes place in the afternoon after the monks have taken their last meal of the day. In 1983 the family of one of the *sangkhārī* members organized this merit-making rite. A gift consisting of a piece of white cloth and money was also presented to the *phāutā* and the two *māechī* during the ceremony.

During the Lent retreat itself there are two other days of important calendrical temple rites. On these days the "returned spirits of the ancestors" (*prēt*) are feasted with food. These rites are conducted some time in September around the ninth and tenth lunar month. The end of the Lent season, in October, calls for another ritual gathering at the temple. This also involves another outdoor *sajbāt* rite similar to the one that marks the first three days of the Lent retreat.

The temple events just mentioned are rites which are determined by precise lunar dates. However, there are other temple ceremonies which are held on certain dates not necessarily determined by the lunar constellation. For instance, gift-giving ceremonies of the *thāut phā pā* kind can be conducted at any time of the year. However, gift-giving ceremonies of the *kathin* type can only be performed within a period of one month immediately after the Lent retreat, but the actual date of the ceremony is not rigidly determined, as in the case of *mākhabūchā* or *wisākhabūchā*.

Apart from the calendrical rites there are also extraordinary temple events. Kelantanese temples regularly hold functions to raise money (*ngān hā bia*) for special projects such as the construction of new sermon buildings, kitchen and dining halls, walls surrounding the temple ground, and the repair of and extension to other monastic buildings. Sometimes a celebration is also held to mark the completion of the construction of such structures. This is basically a dedicatory celebration (*ngān chalāung*), intended to formally donate the finished structure to the *sangha*. In Bān Klāng, the archway that spans the temple entrance became the cause for this kind of celebration in 1983.[6]

The ritual calendar of the village is far from demanding on the residents of Bān Klāng. Major temple ceremonies take place at well-spaced intervals, except during the period just before and after the Lent retreat. Otherwise, the temple remains quiet, and monks and the laity get together only during the weekly rites of the Buddhist Sabbath (*wan phra*), when there is a gathering of the permanent residents of the temple (the monks, the *māechī*, and the *phāutā*) and other members of the village's religious élite such as the *sangkhārī* and the temple "regulars", that is, the few elderly men and women who spend most of their free time at the temple.

At most temple functions, women far outnumber men of those attending. This seems to conform with similar observations in other Theravāda countries of Southeast Asia. The preponderance of women over men at religious gatherings gives the impression that "the more conspicuous practising Buddhists are women rather than men" (Tambiah 1970, pp. 144–45). And it is not unusual for women occasionally to sponsor major merit-making ceremonies. In Bān Klāng, for three successive years (1981, 1982, and 1983) all the sponsors of *kathin* ceremonies were women; and of the three, two were Chinese. The preponderance of women over men among the congregation is even more conspicuous among the Chinese. Chinese women tend to spend more time at the temple than Chinese men (cf. Kershaw 1973, p. 6).

The number attending a temple function is determined by two major factors: the day of the week the event is organized, and whether it also clashes with a similar occasion at neighbouring temples. Temple functions that are held on weekdays attract fewer people than those held over weekend holidays. Some temple functions, because of their exact lunar reckoning, cannot be manipulated so as to fall on weekends. They have to be conducted all the same, and obviously attendance at such events is relatively poor. Many men, because of their commitment especially to work outside the village, cannot attend and the number of women is therefore much larger.

Second, when rituals at temples are held at the same time, fewer people, especially outsiders, are able to attend the ceremony, partly because many people are simultaneously *phuak wat* members of more than one temple. Such clashes in the times of temple functions are unavoidable because rituals such as *mākhabūchā, wisākhabūchā, āsālahabūchā,* and so forth are organized simultaneously at all temples owing to their exact lunar reckoning. On such occasions residents of a particular village attend the function at their respective temple, while outsiders who have no temples of their own may have to make a choice between various temples. Kinship and friendship factors are often influential in making the decision, and outsiders are likely therefore to attend functions at the temple of the village where their relatives or close friends reside, or for that matter wherever their favourite monks are to be found.

Other temple ceremonies such as *thāut kathin, thāut phā pā,* and ordination are not subject to specific lunar dates and therefore may be organized on any day within a stipulated period. *Thāut kathin,* for instance, can be held any time within one month after the end of the Buddhist Lent; *thāut phā pā,* any time throughout the year. They are usually organized during weekend holidays to ensure maximum attendance.

Therefore, one of the organizing principles most temples follow in deciding on the day to hold a function is to avoid possible clashes with similar events held at other temples. Further, the function, if at all possible, should be held over the weekend, which in Kelantan is Friday.[7] A function held on days other than Friday will also clash with working days and consequently the number of people attending will be smaller.

Another aspect of temple functions is that only the high points of the ritual calendar affect the entire congregation or *phuak wat* of Bān Klāng temple. These include the *kathin* occasions (provided that they do not clash with too many of those at other temples) and special occasions such as commemorative or dedicatory celebrations which are organized on special dates to avoid clashes. Smaller events on the calendar, like *wan phra,* do not involve more than the usual core of temple devotees and the religious élite of the village. Slightly bigger events on the calendar, such as *mākhabūchā*, *wisākhabūchā*, and *āsālahabūchā*, entail a larger number of people but not necessarily the whole village, nor would they involve all members of the congregation who live outside the village.

This brings us to a significant point regarding the relationship between temple attendance and ethnic differentiation. During small temple events, like *wan phra*, ethnic differences become most explicit, because those who attend such rituals are mostly Siamese. A typical attendance consists of the clergy and other temple residents, members of the *sangkhārī*, the handful of temple "regulars" and occasionally a few devout outsiders who return to the village for the morning service. Most of these people are Siamese, with the exception, as always, of one or two Chinese who may join the group of worshippers. However, as a general rule Siamese predominate at these small-scale rites and the absence of Chinese is conspicuous. Generally, more women than men attend such ceremonies too. The only few men who are present are mainly members of the temple lay committee.

During slightly bigger ceremonies, such as the feasting of the returned spirits of the dead (*sajprēt* or *sajrān*), the number of Chinese increases considerably, perhaps even equalling that of the Siamese. The number of people present is also often increased by the gathering of outsiders who belong to the temple's congregation. For instance, Chinese from various towns and other settlements may make the trip to their favourite temples on these occasions. Likewise, Siamese who consider Bān Klāng as their place of worship and those who consider the village their ancestral home gather at the temple for the function. Ceremonies of this scale involve a larger number of Bān Klāng's residents and a considerable number of outsiders. In terms of number it is unclear which ethnic group predominates.

During the biggest of the ceremonies, the Chinese are made quite conspicuous not only by their large presence but also by their generosity in the sponsorship of the ceremony. On these occasions one can expect to see other Chinese as well, especially those who do not normally belong to the temple's congregation, but who are nevertheless invited as the sponsors' guests.

To illustrate this point described above, the rest of this chapter discusses two temple events, one indicative of the simplest of the ceremonies in which the Siamese predominate, the other a slightly larger one in which both Chinese and Siamese members of the community and the congregation participate.

The Buddhist Sabbath

The Buddhist Sabbath (*wan phra*) is a regular event in Bān Klāng that takes place four times every lunar month (the eighth and the fifteenth day of the waxing moon, and the eighth and the fourteenth or fifteenth day of the waning moon) but only a small number of people participate in it. Usually, elderly people of either sex go to the temple for a short morning service, which marks the day. With the exception of one or two elderly Chinese, most of the rest are Siamese residents of the village. The ritual is conducted just after the monks have taken their morning meal, at about eight o'clock. The main part of the ritual consists of the laity asking for and receiving the eight precepts. As most of the laity who follow this rite are old folks with few family responsibilities, they normally spend the rest of the day at the temple reading religious texts or talking to the monks. Some may find the comfort of the temple surroundings ideal for an afternoon nap in unoccupied cubicles or at the pavilion (*sālā*).

Regarding the observance of the eight precepts, more people are involved when the Sabbath coincides with any of the major celebrations listed in Tables 5.1 and 5.2. Otherwise, Sabbath rituals held on days other than these festive occasions tend to lack the spirited atmosphere, partly because the number of those involved in the morning service is very small, rarely exceeding fifteen people, and partly because the occasion does not entail the gathering of people other than the temple "regulars", consisting of ten or so elderly people,[8] the five *sangkhān* members, and occasionally one or two outsiders who make the special trip to attend the morning rite. As usual, no regular pattern of attendance may be discerned in the participation of outsiders in the *wan phra* rite held on normal days. Occasionally, people who now reside outside the village but who still consider themselves *phuak wat* of Bān Klāng's temple attend the morning service. These are usually elderly men and women, mostly Siamese but occasionally also some Chinese from various settlements in the district. Hence, Buddhist Sabbath rites held on normal days usually involve people who are already an integral part of the temple scenario, the "regulars" so to speak. Conspicuous is the absence of many people usually seen during major ceremonies.

Despite the quietude which characterizes Buddhist Sabbath observances in Bān Klāng, two important points should be mentioned here. First, on these days Bān Klāng's second temple which remains desolate most of the time bursts into lively activity. About four or five elderly people gather at this temple in the morning waiting for the monks from the main temple to come by and conduct the service to observe the Buddhist Sabbath. The monks make a special effort to conduct this service at the second temple for the sake of these people who find attendance there more convenient than at the main temple, which is quite a distance away.

The second important point about Buddhist Sabbath observances is that in normal circumstances it is the laity who go to meet the monks and not the monks the laity. Since the temple complex is located quite a distance from the settled area of the village and since the monks are compelled to keep to the minimum their interaction with villagers outside the temple boundary, it is the villagers who visit them and not they the villagers (cf. Tambiah 1970, p. 9). However, not everyone can do just that; because of illness or old age, some of the laity are confined to their homes. In such a case the monks visit them instead, to conduct the *wan phra* rite. In Bān Klāng, monks visit these people regularly during the Buddhist Sabbaths soon after the end of the service at the main and the second temples.

The extension of ritual services to the sick and the aged is not unique to Bān Klāng. Whenever monks visit the Siamese village of Pok Kiang in northern Terengganu, they also make an effort to visit lay people who are confined to their homes owing to sickness or old age. As there is no temple in Pok Kiang the laity gather at the village's monastic residence (*sālā phak song*) to make merit and participate in the rituals at which the visiting monks officiate. Soon after the service at the *sālā*, one or two monks visit these infirm people to conduct the rituals to ask for the five precepts, or if it is a Buddhist Sabbath, the eight precepts, in the comfort of the laity's home, though in a form much abbreviated. Evidently, conscious effort is made to observe the Buddhist Sabbath, even to the extent of making this alternative arrangement whenever possible.

Feasting of the Prēt

During the tenth lunar month (about September) there are two occasions of merit-making for the "returned spirits of the dead" (*prēt*). These occasions are held twice during the month, first on the full moon and then fifteen days later. During the lunar leap year (*athikamāt*) an additional occasion is held for the same kind of rite. Altogether there are three occasions; the first on the fourteenth day of the waning moon of the ninth lunar month (that is, the last day of the ninth lunar month). The other two are held exactly on the same days as in the normal lunar year (see Tables 5.1 and 5.2).

The main part of the ritual entails food offering to a kind of ancestral spirit called *prēt*. There is great variety in the kinds of food offered, but one particular dish is always prepared: one made of glutinous rice that is partially cooked in coconut milk with sugar added, and then tightly wrapped in shoot-leaves of a palm called *palas* (Malay; of the *Licuala* species) and steamed. The Siamese call this food *khāwtom* (Malay: *ketupat*).[9] Other types of food involved are cooked rice, various kinds of sweet cakes, and delicacies. Since the rite usually coincides with the fruit season, the offering also consists of a variety of fruits. However, there is no real limit to the range of food that is offered, but *khāwtom* appears to be closely identified with the *prēt* occasion.[10]

Prēt are associated with the belief that neither rebirth after death nor entry into heaven is immediate. Because of their previous sins the deceased will have to undergo punishment before they can be either admitted into heaven or reborn into the world. Part of this punishment takes the form of having to spend some time in the vicinity of hell until their bad *kamma* is exhausted. These underworld beings are known as *prēt*. Some people consider *prēt* as a kind of ghost or *phī* (*phī chanit neung*) but not as potentially dangerous as an ordinary *phī* and certainly not similar to *winjan* or soul.[11] The general belief is that these *prēt* may be ancestors who are unfortunate enough to be retained close to hell while marking time for their eventual release and rebirth.

The concept behind the *sajprēt* rites seems to be similar to that of the Chinese "Feast of the Hungry Ghosts". In Kelantan it is also known among the Hokkien Chinese as "Dewa Day" and celebrated on the fourteenth day of the seventh Chinese lunar month (Golomb 1978, pp. 167, 216). However, in Bān Klāng no separate occasions are held exclusively by the Chinese residents. Instead they participate fully in the Siamese version of the rite. The only noticeable ritual behaviour that differentiates Chinese from Siamese participants is discernible from the burning of token money by some Chinese women while none of the Siamese do so.[12]

Bān Klāng villagers consider *prēt* to be the spirits of the dead that have been left outside but within the vicinity of hell (*narok*). Their position is precarious. Although they have some good *kamma*, this is not enough to warrant them a place in heaven (*sawan*), for they still have some demerit (*bāp*) or bad *kamma*, which must be paid for first. Yet the same bad *kamma* is not serious enough for them to be placed in hell. Hence *prēt* are supposed to mark time within the vicinity of hell until their bad *kamma* (*kam chua*) has worn off.

Although the *prēt* are believed to be confined to underworld dwellings, they are, however, released during the tenth lunar month and permitted to return to their surviving families to receive food from them. During this time a returning *prēt* may observe the goings-on among living family members. What concerns *prēt* most is whether they are leading a proper and fruitful life or whether they are wasting away their worldly existence, merely consuming the material goods the *prēt* left behind without doing anything much to gain further merit by putting their inheritance to good use.

Upon returning to their former villages, the *prēt*, seated on tree branches close to their former houses and on roof rafters, observe all that is happening among their descendants (*lūklān*). Other favourite haunts of the *prēt* are the crossroads and paths of the village. Occasionally, a *prēt*, unsatisfied with the kind of worldly preoccupation its descendants are involved in, may inflict upon them illness to express its disapproval and anger. When a strange sickness, such as the rare yellow fever, unexpectedly strikes a family member around this time of the year, the misfortune is attributed to the curse of the displeased *prēt*.

During the tenth lunar month, the released *prēt* enjoy various kinds of merit made in their names. To feed the returning ancestors, villagers as always reserve two separate days for holding the rituals of food offerings to the *prēt*. A number of terms are used to refer to these occasions. The more general one is *sajprēt*, but other terms include *sajrān* and *songrān*. These terms require a little elaboration here: *sajprēt* means putting something out for the *prēt*. A small platform used to place these offerings is called *rān*, hence the name *sajrān* (putting something on the platform). The two terms are used interchangeably, and when one talks about *sajrān* or *sajprēt* one refers to the special ritual offering conducted during the tenth lunar month. As mentioned, there are two occasions for this during the usual lunar year, but three during the lunar leap year. Another term, *songrān*, is also used, but it refers specifically to the very last in the series of two ritual events (in the case of a normal lunar year) or three (in the case of a lunar leap year). The word *song*, meaning "to send something away", is used by villagers to signify that the *prēt*, after being feasted by their surviving descendants, are now returning to their dwelling at the close of the tenth lunar month.

On the day preceding a performance of either *sajrān* or *songrān* two platforms are constructed by the villagers, one inside and another outside the temple compound. The first is called *rān naj* ("inner platform"), the second, built close to the main entrance, is called *rān nōk* ("outer platform"). Each is about 1.5 metres high with a floor area of about 1.5 metres by 1 metre. Both are made of wooden planks raised on poles. The floor is lined with freshly cut banana leaves (*bajtāung, bajtonkluaj*). At one corner of the floor an open black umbrella is placed, its handle tied to one of the four poles supporting the *rān* structure. Under the umbrella are placed a kettle (or a large mug) of tea (*nāmchā*) and a young coconut, a small section of its top sliced off a little to expose the juice and the flesh inside. It is believed that the three items will attract the *prēt* to the *rān* because under the hot tropical sun nothing looks more inviting than the shade of an open umbrella, a container of cooling tea, and a fresh young coconut. There is a mock ladder made from the mid-rib of banana leaf (*kāntāung*) leading from the ground up to the floor of the *rān* (for the *prēt* to climb the *rān* and feast on the offering). Building the second *rān* outside the temple compound is absolutely necessary since some *prēt*, due to the nature of their previous sins, could not gain any entry into the temple grounds. On the actual day of the *sajrān*, a special chant read by the monks will summon the *prēt* to come and relish the offering of food and to rejoice in the merit-making.

A yellow cord (*sājsīn*) is secured to the tip of the umbrella fixed to the outside *rān*. This cord is then passed and tied to the tip of the other umbrella on the second *rān* inside the temple compound. From there it is led into the sermon hall (*māe wat*), where it is wound around an image of the Buddha, after which it is passed in front of a row of seated monks, each of whom holds the cord between the palms of their hands, which are pressed together. The cord ends in a small ball placed by the side of the last monk in the row. The string, it is explained, will carry the merit and the magical charge from the Buddha image and the chanting monks to the two *rān* outside the sermon hall and then to the *prēt* feasting on the offerings.[13]

The actual ceremony of food offering to the *prēt* does not normally begin until just before noon. People start to gather within the temple compound early in the morning of the appointed day. Those from distant places will already have arrived in the village the day before and perhaps have spent the night in the temple itself or with relatives in the village. The monks themselves, however, begin the day's ceremony well before noon. Just after finishing their morning meal (*chan chāw*) they gather inside the ordination hall to do the chanting (*suat*) specially for the *prēt*. No lay person is involved in this.

At about 9.30 a.m. a drum is sounded to call villagers who are not already at the temple to proceed there as the offering of food to the *prēt* is about to begin. The time between the first sounding of the drum and the ceremony itself is quite a lengthy period. So there is no sudden rush of people to the temple, but rather a steady, unhurried flow of men, women, and children streaming into the temple compound and filling whatever space is still available in the sermon hall. Almost every female person present carries along various containers of food and other items to be offered to the monks and the *prēt*. At about 10.30 a.m., when most of the people have already arrived, the first sequence of the ceremony begins. This takes the form of the customary *wāj phra* and the asking and receiving of the five precepts (and, where appropriate, the asking for and the receiving of the eight precepts).[14] As usual this is done with one of the *sangkhārī* members acting as the ritual leader (*phūnam*). This done, the monks read a chant (known as *suat hajphāun*), which incorporates a blessing for the congregation.

While the monks are chanting, the crowd forms a queue in the middle of the hall, with women at the start of the queue, in order to perform the *sajbāt* rite, wherein spoonfuls of cooked rice are placed into various containers consisting of a large basin and a number of alms bowls. After this the same people proceed to the two *rān* to present their offerings of rice and other food items to the *prēt*. This takes quite a while before everyone has done so. Meanwhile, the monks continue with the chanting.

It is at this particular stage of the ritual sequence that some, but not all, Chinese participants may distinguish themselves from the rest of the congregation. They take turns burning token money (normally used during Chinese funeral ceremonies) at the base of each platform. In contrast, none of the Siamese present do this.

Those who have placed their offerings of food on the two platforms then return to the sermon hall. This marks the beginning of the next phase of the ceremony. One of the *sangkhārī* members, this time the *ācān wat* acting as the lay ritual leader (*phūnam*), leads the congregation in intoning the formula of offering (*khāthā thawāj*) to the monks and the *prēt*. The essence of this act is to dedicate the food to the benefit of the members of the *sangha*, the *prēt*, and other beings whether visible or otherwise that may be present within the temple's precincts. The congregation also asks for the merit to be transferred to the *prēt* as well as to deceased parents, ancestors, and relatives.

The offering ceremony completed, the monks read a chant called *anumōthanā khāthā* to bless the presentation of food and gifts. As soon as this finishes, members of the congregation read a special formula, called *truatnām*,[15] in which once again the lay congregation seeks the transfer of merit to the *prēt* and other beings worthy of rejoicing in the merit thus made.

As soon as this is over, one of the *sangkhārī* members takes a basket which contains a number of small balls made of woven green coconut leaves (*lūk krapau*) and throws them to the waiting crowd of children already milling around in anticipation outside the sermon hall. This proves to be an expected treat for the children because enclosed in these balls are coins amounting from twenty to fifty cents. There is normally quite a tussle among the children as they elbow and push each other for these balls.[16] For this particular occasion these balls were made by one of the *māechī* of Bān Klāng temple; the coins used were her contribution to the merit-making occasion.

After the chanting, the *thawāj* ceremony, and the throwing of the balls, the monks descend from the higher level of the hall in order to take their last meal of the day. By this time trays of food brought by households and others from outside the village have already been laid out and each of the monks takes his place to eat. Since there is a large number of trays as usual, each monk is offered between four and five trays of food. Members of the *sangkhārī* and a few lay members of the congregation are the only ones who hand over the

trays of food to the monks, while female members of the congregation who have been previously busy arranging the food in the trays
watch the procedure from a distance. A monk, upon being presented
with the trays, touches their edges to symbolize his acceptance of the
food. He does not eat everything in the trays offered him but rather
concentrates on just one, while taking bits and pieces from other trays
every now and then. The *sangkhārī* and a few lay members wait on
the monks as they eat, seeing to their need for drinking water, spittoons, and glasses, among other things.

After the monks have finished with their meal, they read another
short chant and then take leave to retire for the afternoon to their
quarters. Some monks make themselves available for a brief audience
with members of the lay congregation. Many of those whom the
monks talk to at this particular moment are also relatives and friends
who have come from distant places.

As soon as the monks have finished eating, the trays of food are
claimed by their respective owners, who repack whatever is left into
containers. These are taken home, but some trays, often with food
hardly touched, are passed on to various groups in the congregation.
As this day in 1982 fell on the Buddhist Sabbath (*wan phra*), some of
the congregation members resolved to observe the eight precepts.
Since one of these precepts requires abstinence from eating after
mid-day, they must eat as soon as possible before noon, and do so
immediately after the monks have finished eating.

While the monks are still eating, children begin to mill around
the two platforms, getting ready to help themselves to the offerings
that are placed on them. The stampede to retrieve a share of the
offerings begins when it is announced that the monks have finished
with their morning meals. Some energetic children even climb right
up onto the platform itself. The more energetic younger adults may
also join in the scramble for the offerings, and whatever can be
salvaged from the two platforms is filled into baskets and plastic bags.
The whole platform is cleared of everything, except for the umbrella,
the young coconut, and the container of tea (*nāmchā*) within a matter
of minutes. Food that is spilt onto the ground is picked up by dogs,
which move in as soon as the area around the platform is clear of
people.

For ordinary members of the congregation, this concludes the
day's event of feasting the *prēt*. The *sangkhārī* members, however, stay

behind since a few more things need to be attended to. They gather at one corner of the sermon hall to count the money received during the day's ceremony. This is the *anumōthanā* money donated by members of the congregation, typically by outsiders and visitors, at various times in the morning just before the *sajbāt* and *sajrān* rites. Usually a monk's bowl to receive contributions is placed at the foot of the image of the Buddha. The contents of this bowl are emptied and counted at the conclusion of the day's ritual, usually just after the monks have finished eating. The amount collected is then divided equally according to the number of monks officiating at the ritual. Each share is wrapped in newspaper or in a page torn off from a used calendar. These packets are then distributed to the monks by slipping them into their shoulder bags.

NOTES

1. The tree is a significant symbol in Buddhism. Referring to northeast Thailand, Tambiah (1970, p. 165) attributes these trees to a Buddhist symbolism perhaps unknown to the villagers. They appear to resemble the "trees that gratify the desires of men" (*Kalpavriksha*). In popular Buddhism they are said to represent "the four trees that will blossom at the four corners of the city in which the next Buddha, Maitreya, will be born. They will then produce all kinds of delicious fruits in fabulous quantities" (ibid.). Terwiel associates this symbolism with the heavenly *kapparukkha* trees "which reputedly yield any object individuals may wish them to yield" (1979, p. 239).

2. The stepped area and the altar are respectively locations no. 2 and no. 4 in Figure 4.2. The stepped area forms a physical divide between the monks and the laymen during most ritual occasions. It can be considered as some kind of transitional area where gift items are placed and displayed before being eventually presented to the monks. During the course of a ritual no one, not even the monks, sits in this part of the hall. As a general rule should a monk need to approach the laity, the stepped area is the lowest point to which he would descend.

3. Siamese residents of Bān Klāng even think that some of their customs and traditions (*praphēnī*) may not be the same as those prevalent in Thailand but add that the closest similarities, perhaps, are southern Thailand (*phāktāj*). Even between various Siamese villages in Kelantan

there are differences in the details of conducting the same rituals. In addition, there exist dialect differences between Siamese villages in Kelantan (Kershaw 1969, p. 81).

4. *Athikamāt* is the Siamese leap year of lunar reckoning, usually indicated in the Siamese calendar by an extra eighth month. Skinner mentions that although the Siamese calendar is based on the lunar year it is nevertheless adjusted to the solar calendar by inserting "an extra 'thirteenth month' once every three years, intercalated after the normal eighth month" (1965, p. 156). The ninth month follows as usual. Wyatt also makes a mention of this old luni-solar calendar (1974, p. 16, n. 49).

5. For more details on *prēt*, see the section below on "Feasting of the *Prēt*".

6. This celebration is described in detail in Chapter 7.

7. Unlike in most of the west coast states, in Kelantan the working week for government departments and large businesses begins on Saturday and continues to Thursday afternoon, Thursday being a half working day. The weekend starts from Thursday afternoon and continues into the whole of Friday.

8. These are mainly people, both men and women, who lead a semi-retired life and depend on the support of their grown-up children or relatives. They while away most of their time at the temple helping the monks with various chores.

9. This is quite different from the *ketupat* that one usually finds in the west coast states, where they are made from ordinary white rice, boiled in small rectangular-shaped packets woven from shoot-leaves of the coconut tree. While both the Kelantanese and the west coast versions are generally known as *ketupat*, in Kelantan the term refers specifically to the one that is made from glutinous rice and "wrapped" in *palas* leaves whereas the one that is made from ordinary rice and "wrapped" in shoot-leaves of the coconut palm is known as *ketupat nasi*.

10. As a comparison, in Malay oral tradition *ketupat* is associated with food that one takes along when embarking on a long journey, since it keeps for many days quite easily. It is most appropriate too for the *prēt* to be offered the same kind of food because of the presumably long journey they take from an underworld abode to the village.

11. Davis (1984, pp. 61, 75) explains that in folk Buddhism all persons are believed to become *prēt* immediately upon their death and are then reborn into some other forms of existence. In one sense, according to Davis, *prēt* are recently deceased, but in another, they are "a particular form of spirit (*phī*) which suffers constant thirst and hunger because

its tiny mouth cannot take in enough sustenance to nourish its tall and emanciated body". Davis adds further that *prēt* in this latter sense "are given to making nocturnal appearances, especially on the night of full moon and new moon. They are frightening, but harmless" (ibid., p. 76).

According to Buddhist cosmology, *prēt* occupy one of the five Worlds of Desire. The five consist of the following, starting from the lowest:

(a) Hell (*Narok*; Pali: *Niraya*)
(b) Sphere of Animals (Pali: *tiracchānabhūmi*)
(c) Sphere of Ghosts (Pali: *petavisayabhūmi*)
(d) Sphere of Demons (Pali: *asurakāyabhūmi*)
(e) Sphere of Human Beings (Pali: *manussabhūmi*)

Into the last four of these levels of existence are born people whose misdeeds outweigh their good deeds (Davis 1984, p. 75). The level which the *prēt* occupy (the third in the order above) is slightly higher than that of the animal, but lower than that of the demons. Davis uses the term *preta*. For more details on this, see, for instance, Davis (1984, pp. 75–77) and Schumann (1973, p. 51). See also Reynolds (1976, pp. 204, 205).

12. For accounts of the Chinese version of the festival, see DeBernardi (1984); see also Purcell (1948, pp. 126–27) and Maeda (1967, p. 77).

13. Tambiah (1970, p. 159) gives a slightly different interpretation with regard to the ritual significance of the cord. According to him the cord encloses all people within the boundary of a merit-making activity, enabling them to acquire the merit so generated. In any case the cord may still be seen as the conduit of magical power and merit in the ceremony.

14. This rite precedes most ceremonies at the temples and prepares the congregation for the ceremony immediately following. Terwiel (1979, p. 188) interprets this as a ritual act of cleansing, a purification which enables the laymen to receive the benefits of ceremony in a proper manner. The villagers explain that this ritual prelude puts one in the purest state of mind a layman can achieve.

15. For a typical text of this formula, see, for instance, Wells (1975, pp. 119, 120).

16. The throwing of these coconut-leaf balls is quite common during temple ceremonies. In the village where Golomb did his field-work the money is contained in balls made of banana leaf instead of coconut leaf. The people in this village called these balls *luug kamphryg* (Golomb 1978, p. 168). I could not find the equivalent of this term in standard

Thai; perhaps it is the local pronunciation of *lūk krapau*, meaning "bulb", or "something having the shape of a bulb", which the coconut-leaf balls resemble. Sometimes no coconut-leaf balls are used; instead, handfuls of bare coins are thrown among the waiting children.

Chapter 6
The Kathin Ceremony

The *kathin* ceremony is one of the most important events; it not only proclaims the end of the Lent season for the monks but also marks the special month of merit-making for the laity. It also highlights the change of mood from "ascetic" Buddhism observed during Lent to "festive" Buddhism which is associated with temple fairs and celebrations.[1] When monks come out of their retreat the laity organize feasts for them and offer them gifts of cloth and other useful items. The *kathin* thus provides the opportunity for the laity to make merit. Gift-giving during this month is believed to generate more merit than at other times of the year; the most meritorious of acts is the sponsorship of the *kathin* occasion itself (cf. Terwiel 1979, p. 215).

Kathin celebrations take place during the month immediately following the Lent retreat (*phansā*), usually in October. The last of the retreat itself ends on the fifteenth day of the waxing moon of the eleventh lunar month. In terms of the Siamese lunar calendar, the *kathin* season starts from the first day of the waning half of the eleventh month to the fifteenth day of the waxing moon of the twelfth lunar month. The highlight of the event is the presentation (*thawāj*) of yellow robes to the monks. However, on most occasions the symbolic significance of the yellow robes is overshadowed by other gift items, known as *khryangbāuriwān*, particularly the "accessory items" and money-trees whose total cost surpasses that of the sets of yellow cloth. A similar observation of the ceremony in Thailand was made by Davis (1984, p. 200) regarding the robes: they now no longer command the ritual focus of the ceremony, but are "overshadowed" by other gifts including large sums of money.

The actual cost of holding of a *kathin* ritual can be tremendous. Terwiel mentions that one of the main reasons the *kathin* ceremony carries great prestige and honour to the main sponsor is that it is extremely expensive (1979, p. 237). However, because the spiritual and social rewards outweigh the expenses involved, there is never a real shortage of potential sponsors. In fact, many wealthy members of the congregation, typically the Chinese, compete with one another to be the sponsor. As a result many temples have a long waiting list of future sponsors for each year's *kathin*. A wait of two to three years is quite common, or even five years in temples with a large number of supporters.

According to local belief, the most significant thing about *kathin* is that the store of merit it generates will be more than enough to ensure the sponsor a better rebirth and future life. The high social prestige accruing to the sponsor is further enhanced by the limited opportunity available for staging *kathin* ceremonies, which may be held only once a year by any temple, solely within the month immediately after the Lent retreat (*phansā*). One could of course make a valuable presentation to the monks at other times of the year, but the merit and the social dividends from doing so are incomparable with the rewards of a *kathin* presentation. A gift-giving ceremony held outside the *kathin* month is technically known as *thāut phā pā* (literally, "to lay the cloth in the forest", being a reference to the practice of ancient monks who went around collecting discarded pieces of cloth, especially from burial sites, to be used for monastic robes). Unlike *kathin*, a *thāut phā pā* can be conducted at any time of the year, even during the *kathin* month itself.

Kathin ceremonies occasion the gathering and mobilization of the temple's *phuak wat* for the purpose of merit-making. They also draw in outsiders who do not normally belong to the congregation but who nevertheless are invited to the function by the sponsors. In many cases the sponsors of *kathin* are outsiders. Many factors are taken into consideration in the selection of sponsors, kinship being decidedly one of them. For instance, the sponsors of *kathin* ceremonies in Bān Klāng during 1982, 1983, and 1984 were outsiders to the village but regular members of the temple's *phuak wat*. Two of these sponsors were women, one Chinese, the other Siamese. One thing they had in common was that they had close relatives living in the village. The sponsor for the 1984 *kathin* was a Siamese man who lived in Pok

Kiang, a Siamese settlement without a temple in northern Terengganu. Not only did both of his parents live in Bān Klāng, but his wife's
father, who was a monk, resided at the temple of the village.[2] Whereas
in Thailand it is quite usual for the *kathin* ceremonies to be sponsored
by government agencies and private companies (Davis 1984, p. 200),
in Kelantan many wealthy families, including Chinese ones, undertake the sponsorship instead. Some of these Chinese are not necessarily residents of Bān Klāng. Nevertheless, they provide support to
the temple because of the kin connections that many have in the
village. Evidently, sponsoring temple functions is one way of express-
ing their desire to maintain links with the ancestors of their village,
apart from other considerations.

Generally in Kelantan, there are two types of *kathin* ceremonies,
the main difference between them being in the nature of their
sponsorship. If a *kathin* ceremony is sponsored by an individual or a
family, then it is known as a "private" *kathin* (*kathin cawphāp, kathin
cawkhāung*). In contrast, if the *kathin* has no individual sponsor, but
is organized collectively by the villagers and outside members of the
phuak wat, the occasion is called a "public" *kathin* (*kathin sāmakkhī*).

Because of the large number of potential sponsors available each
year the private type of *kathin* is most common, yet some temples have
occasionally dispensed with privately sponsored *kathin*. The main
reason for this is quite complex and needs some elaboration here.
In the case of a privately sponsored *kathin* the greater part of the
merit accrues to an individual as well as to his or her immediate family
members; others attending may gain some merit too, but not as
much. On the other hand, in a publicly sponsored *kathin* the merit
is believed to be equally distributed to everyone taking part in the
ceremony. Further, some abbots and temple steering committees are
known to discourage individual *kathin* sponsorship specifically to
prevent discord within the community and the congregation, particularly when fierce competition between contending sponsors is
anticipated. A good solution is to organize it on a public basis without
any individual sponsorship. The occasion is thereby credited, as is the
merit equally distributed, to the entire community and to all the
congregation members who participate in the ritual.[3]

The sponsor of a private *kathin* is known as the "host" (*cawphāp*)
or the "owner" (*cawkhāung*). This compares with a public *kathin*,
which does not have anyone in particular as host. Because of this,

public *kathin* becomes an open, free-for-all affair, since everyone can make his contribution to the array of gifts meant for the monastic institution. This is not to say that fewer people attend a private *kathin.* Attendance at either may be equally large, but normally the public just do not feel as free to turn up at a private *kathin* without having been invited by the sponsor. The same people would not hesitate, however, to attend any publicly sponsored *kathin,* at whichever temple it is held, because of the "open nature" of the occasion.

Therefore any thoughtful sponsor of a private *kathin* would be quite mindful of this. If the *kathin* is to be a success the sponsor has to pay meticulous attention when drawing up the guest list to ensure that as many people as possible are invited to the ceremony and that no one that the *cawphāp* knows is overlooked. Invitations are therefore extended as widely as possible; but one simple way of doing this is to delegate the responsibility to the steering committee (*sangkhārī*) of the temple at which the *kathin* is to be held. The response to both personal and delegated invitations is usually good. The chances are that the guests who eventually turn up will be the same persons whose *kathin* (or other religious or social undertakings) the sponsor had previously been invited to and attended.

Another difference between the two types of *kathin* relates to the money collected during the course of the celebration. It is customary for those who attend the day's ceremony to make a small contribution towards the cost of organizing the ceremony. A container is usually placed strategically in the sermon hall for collecting the cash donation; a used monk's bowl (*bāt*) often makes an ideal receptacle. At the conclusion of the day's ritual, this contribution, called *anumōthanā* money, is counted. If the *kathin* ceremony is of the private kind, all the money collected in the receptacle rightfully belongs to the sponsor (*khyn cawphāp*) rather than to the temple. Since the *cawphāp* has already made a considerable cash outlay to finance the ceremony he or she has the right to keep the day's takings. On the other hand, if sponsorship of the *kathin* is of the public kind, whatever the amount collected as *anumōthanā* money automatically belongs to the temple (*khyn wat*). Normally, private sponsors do not take this money for themselves but instead donate all of it to the temple; doing so distinguishes a magnanimous sponsor from one who operates strictly in accordance with the rule.

The exact date for holding a *kathin,* as for major temple ceremonies, is determined so as to avoid clashes with similar functions in other places, particularly at the nearest temples within the same district.[4] If neighbouring temples were to organize functions on the same day, those who were not members of the temple's congregation would face the difficulty of deciding which temple to attend. It is difficult for a person to be at two or more ceremonies held on the same day because the crucial parts of the ceremony take place simultaneously in the mid-afternoon. Attending one function and missing the other also amounts to choosing between sponsors, a difficult decision given the small and closely knit nature of the local Buddhist population. Because of this, guests whose conspicuous absence may offend the sponsors often endeavour to make token appearances at different functions. They show up at one temple in the morning of the day on which the ceremony is held. After being served with food they hand over their contributions of money to the sponsor or place them in the receptacle provided and, after a polite exchange of small talk, excuse themselves, and rush off to another temple, arriving just in time for the tail end of a similar ceremony.

Generally, a *kathin* is held on a Friday, the weekend holiday, to allow for maximum participation. Preparations for the function begin several days earlier. The day immediately preceding the *kathin* is called "starting day" (*wan roem ngān*); however, there is nothing ritually important about this day, except that all preparations for the occasion must be finalized by then, including last-minute additions of items to the collection of gifts, most of which have already been on display in the sermon hall for several days.

It is on the preceding day, too, that members of the congregation from distant places, particularly those from Narathiwat and the *nikhom* settlements, begin the trip back to their "ancestral village" of Bān Klāng so as to be in time for the ceremony that is due to take place the following day. Others may have arrived a few days earlier to help out with the preparations. It is important that these people be in the village at least one day before the event because of the unreliable public transport. Were they to start their journey back to the village in the morning of the day of the ceremony, the chances are that they would not arrive before mid-afternoon, when the crucial part of the ritual takes place. Hence, by the eve of the appointed day most of the congregation from distant places would already have arrived in the village.

The 1983 Kathin in Bān Klāng

The *kathin* ceremony has been described in detail in the literature[5] but the occasion about to be narrated is quite different from the usual in one particular sense. Originally planned from the very outset as a *kathin* ceremony, it was changed to a *thāut phā pā* due to some last-minute complications. Nevertheless, this particular event illustrates the kind of adjustment temples have to make in the light of the dwindling number of monks who are conversant with details of Buddhist rituals. The case also clearly illustrates the ritual dominance the Siamese have over the Chinese in temple affairs, even though the ceremony itself was sponsored by the latter. For the major part, the preparation for the ceremony and its entire ritual conduct relied heavily upon the involvement of the Siamese, particularly members of their community's religious élite.

The 1983 *kathin* was held on 28 October, and was sponsored by a Chinese woman from Kota Bharu to make merit for her late father. Although she was not a resident of Bān Klāng, many of her close relatives lived in the village. She was typical of those Chinese who make every effort to attend major ceremonies, and her relationship with the temple's monks was close. Sponsorship expenses for the ceremony approximated M$4,000. Part of this went to pay for the cost of food served to guests and members of the congregation. She also spent about M$3,000 on the seven money-trees (*ton ngōen*), which constituted her direct cash donation to the temple. The total value of banknotes pinned on each tree ranged from M$60 to M$200. There were also six trays of yellow cloth, one for each monk of the temple. Later, on the eve of the *kathin*, another tray was added to these six by a relative of the sponsor. The contents of this extra tray became the property of the temple and not of the monks.

Yellow cloth for the monks' garments, the most important item whose absence would make the *kathin* incomplete, was also presented. The cloth was bought in Narathiwat the year before by one of the monks at the request of the sponsor. The same cloth could be bought in Sungai Golok across the border in Thailand, but it would be more expensive.[6] Other presentation items which are ritually important, known as "the eight necessities" (*bāurikānpāet*), were also presented. A set of these consists of a monk's bowl (*bāt*), sewing needles and thread, a pair of slippers, razor blades, water filter, a nail clipper or a small knife, an umbrella, a toothbrush, and a tube of toothpaste.

In addition, other "accessory" items (*khryangbāuriwān*) costing around M$400 were also presented. They comprised an electric fan, two sets of flourescent lamps and tubes, two sets of round dining tables with ten wooden stools, an aluminium kitchen sink, an aluminium kettle, mats, and a kerosene stove. Some of these items were previously given to the sponsor by relatives and friends to be added to the grand collection of *kathin* offering. Some friends and relatives, however, chose to give her money instead, well in advance of the *kathin* day, so that she could buy these additional items herself. Some of the money given her in this way was also used in the making of the "money-trees" (*ton ngōen*). A small gold-plated image of the Buddha, bought in Bangkok for M$1,000 by a relative of the host, was also presented as part of the *khryangbāuriwān*.

The sponsor explained that all the items presented for the *kathin* were collected gradually over the previous year, that is, as soon as she knew that she was selected to be the next sponsor. An intending sponsor for the coming year's *kathin* gets to know whether his or her bid for sponsorship has been successful at the conclusion of the current year's *kathin*. Usually lots are drawn to determine who gets to be the following year's sponsor. Some temples do not draw lots but place the names of all intending sponsors on a waiting list. A year's notice gives the sponsor sufficient time to accumulate the items to be presented, to inform and invite relatives and friends and, most important, to save enough money to finance the undertaking.

Most things to be presented at the *kathin* ceremony were sent to the temple and placed in the care of the temple steering committee (*sangkhārī*) during the week before the ceremony. Larger "accessory" items such as tables, chairs, kitchen sink, and so forth had been delivered even earlier. During the few weeks preceding the *kathin* day the sponsor visited the temple regularly to check final details of the arrangements and to consult with the monks and the *sangkhārī* members. Arrangements for cooking and waiting duties on the day of the function were also worked out by the *sangkhārī* members. It was not difficult to look for people to do the job, as there were often many volunteers, both village residents and outsiders.

No single person actually administered and supervised these tasks. No detailed directives were issued with military-like authority, not

even by the *sangkhārī* members or the highest person in the religious
hierarchy of the temple. Yet everybody seemed to know exactly how
to make himself useful, and things were done with an unobtrusive
efficiency by everyone involved; if there were cups, glasses, kettles,
spittoons, plates, and serving containers that needed washing — after
having collected dust in the temple's storerooms — they were washed
and arranged at proper places in the temple kitchen, ready for use;
if the food serving area was full of rubbish it was swept clean; if chairs
and tables were still in the storage area they were taken out, dusted,
and laid out where required; if the cooking sheds needed repair this
was done almost instantly by the person who first noticed that they
called for repair; if the firewood supply was insufficient it was
replenished almost immediately; and if the water tank was empty, no
time was wasted in starting up the pump. The buzz of activity was
orderly; everyone knew that a big celebration was on the way.

The last few days approaching the *kathin* saw some members of
the village community and others of the wider congregation becoming more involved, but not frantic, in helping in whatever way they
could. Women, both Siamese and Chinese, provided the main source
of labour. While most were residents of Bān Klāng, it was not uncommon for outsiders to come and help as well, especially those who
belonged to the wider congregation of *phuak wat* and those who were,
at the same time, friends and relatives of the sponsor. A festive
atmosphere prevailed, but there was also much work to be done.
However, with so many helping hands around, no task was too
onerous. These activities gained momentum as the *kathin* day
approached.

Three days before the appointed day, friends and relatives of the
sponsor started preparing the large amount of food to be served to
guests. Since the 1983 sponsor was not a resident of Bān Klāng the
preparation took place at the house of her relatives in the village. Fish
was bought in huge quantities and delivered to the house where
relatives, neighbours, and friends helped with the gutting, cleaning,
and cooking.[7] Apart from the fish, vegetables were also prepared by
the same group of people. Bags of rice, sugar, milk, tea, coffee, and
syrups, bought two or three days earlier, were sent for temporary
storage in the kitchen of the temple until the *kathin* day.

The monks and the two *māechī* together with other *sangkhārī*
members helped to display the gift items in the sermon hall. Elderly

women of the village came in the evenings to lend a helping hand wrapping and decorating the items to be presented. The money-trees were made in the sponsor's house and delivered to the temple on the eve of the celebration. By the evening of the same day most of the gift items had been deposited at the temple and arranged on the stepped area of the sermon hall in readiness for the following day's ceremony. The whole collection looked somewhat ostentatious but this was exactly as intended. Villagers, guests, and those who had just arrived from distant places came to admire the display. The host sat in one corner of the sermon hall and talked with her guests until the early hours of the morning.

The Day of the Kathin

Activities on the *kathin* day itself started very early. People who had been assigned cooking duties arrived at daybreak to cook the rice and heat the accompanying dishes (*kabkhāw*) that were prepared a few days earlier. Some of the food was served to monks as their morning meal since on a special day like this, no households are on roster to bring food for the monks.

The morning also saw the arrival of more of the sponsor's guests and relatives from various places. As usual there was a steady stream of people coming to the temple; they first went into the sermon hall where the host received them. After an exchange of small talk, guests handed over some cash donation (*anumōthanā* money) to the sponsor. Sometimes the money was not directly handed to the host but was instead deposited into a container positioned next to the collection of *kathin* gifts. The purpose of such donations is to defray the cost involved in the sponsorship as well as to generate merit for the giver.

After briefly meeting the sponsor, the guests were ushered towards the kitchen of the temple, where they were seated at the tables and served a meal of rice and relishes, iced drinks, and sweet cakes. After eating, they were free to do anything they pleased since the gift-giving rite, the day's climax, would not begin until mid-afternoon. Meanwhile, people who had arrived earlier settled themselves in the monks' empty quarters, on the pavilion (*sālā*) in the temple compound, and in the sermon hall itself, mostly talking to one another, exchanging news and renewing old acquaintances. People who had been invited by the sponsor continued streaming in and the same

procedure of receiving them and serving them with food was repeated over and over again. As Bān Klāng was not the only temple
where such a function was taking place that day, some guests had
to leave early for similar functions at other villages. Hence, by late
morning, there was a constant flow of people in and out, engaging
in small talk as they meet at the temple gate. Even as the crucial part
of the ceremony was about to begin, people were still arriving.

The next part of the day's ceremony was the procession of gift
items. Presumably this was the most colourful and perhaps the
noisiest event of the day; colourful because nearly all the items,
except the heaviest and the bulkiest, were taken off from the display
area and put on parade; noisiest because the parade was accom-
panied by a group of musicians playing loudly the usual Siamese
festival music on percussion instruments. Most of those present
selected something from the collection and carried it to a marshalling
point, a pavilion (*sālā*) located at the junction of the main road of
the village and the access road to the temple. The trays of yellow
cloth, the money-trees, and other lighter items were carried by the
women, who formed the majority in the procession. The men and
the stronger children helped to carry heavier items. Others also
joined in the procession even if they were not carrying anything.
Because of the procession, this day of *kathin* is also known as the
"procession day" (*wan hāe kathin*).

Led by a man carrying a triangular yellow flag and the musicians,
the procession made its way along the approach road to the temple.
On entering the temple ground, it circled the ordination hall three
times before making its way into the sermon hall. Monks did not join
in the procession but awaited its arrival, sitting on the raised section
of the sermon hall, ready for the rite of presentation. People who
were carrying the gifts proceeded to the stepped area and after posit-
ioning them in appropriate places, sat themselves on the floor facing
the monks. By then glasses of iced drink were passed to everyone in
the congregation by a number of women who had not joined the
procession but stayed behind to help prepare the refreshments. The
drinks were much appreciated since the procession had taken place
under the hot afternoon sun.

The next phase of the ceremony differed dramatically from the
boisterousness of previous proceedings. Perhaps sped up by the
rounds of iced drink passed, an atmosphere of quietude and serious-

ness descended, as the lay ritual leader (*phūnam*), who was also one of the *sangkhārī* members, took up position to lead the congregation, professing homage to the Buddha, followed by the rite of seeking refuge in the three symbolic elements of Theravāda Buddhism (*phraratanatraj*) — the Buddha, the *dhamma*, and the *sangha*. The deputy abbot, representing the clergy, dispensed this formula phrase by phrase, each repeated by members of the congregation. After the formula of refuge was said three times, the five precepts were uttered by the monk and repeated by the congregation. To request and receive the five precepts is believed to put the lay congregation in a state of spiritual purity and readiness for the gift-giving rite which was about to begin.

The next stage was the presentation of the offering (*thawāj khryangthān*), with the laity saying appropriate formula (*khāthā thawājphra*). However, there was to be a change in that day's proceedings. The deputy abbot waved his hand to the leader of the congregation, (*phūnam*) who then hurriedly approached the monks on the upper level. After a brief exchange of words with them, he returned quickly to the lower level, and looking very concerned whispered something into the ears of other *sangkhārī* members, who seemed quite surprised too. Soon after, the deputy abbot stood up to address the congregation. He apologized to the congregation and especially to the sponsor because the gift-giving ceremony for that day would have to proceed in the form of a *thāut phā pā* presentation instead of a *thāut kathin*. He also explained why the change was necessary: the abbot was not well, and the *krānkathin* rite, the most crucial element of a *kathin* ceremony, could not be performed.

This point requires some elaboration here. In the normal course of a *kathin* proceeding, the ceremony ends with a ritual procedure called *krānkathin* during which the yellow cloth given by the laity is assigned to a particular monk to be made into yellow robes (Wells 1975, pp. 173–78). But most importantly the chanting of a special *suat*, called *suat apphalōk*, must be done, the responsibility for this usually falling upon the most senior monk. Apparently, not many monks know the *suat* by heart, but most monks of a few years' standing should be able to recite the chant after a quick refresh of their memory.

In the case of Bān Klāng it seemed that the abbot was the only one familiar with this particular *suat*. It was also obvious that no one had really anticipated that he would stop short of reading the *suat* on the appointed day. Neither did he warn other monks of the possibility of his illness getting in the way, otherwise contingency measures would have been taken. Since this was a last-minute glitch, the other monks were not quite ready to take over the reading, mainly because hardly any of them knew the *suat* by heart. Hence, the gift-giving ceremony in the form of a *kathin* ceremony could not proceed as originally planned, but the sudden shift was not taken as a major disaster by anyone.

The majority of the lay crowd seemed oblivious to the sudden change in the ritual emphasis. Most continued to whisper to one another even when the deputy abbot was making the announcement, nor was there any visible reaction from the sponsor. Only a few, including the *sangkhārī* members, seemed to understand the implications of the drastic shift in the emphasis of the ritual. Nevertheless, the deputy abbot convinced the crowd that despite the slight change the ceremony remained basically the same. Among other things, he stressed that what mattered most in any merit-making ceremony was the good intention of the giver rather than the form the ceremony should take. That the deputy abbot had a prior consultation with the *phūnam* before making the announcement meant that the ritual leader was required to make appropriate changes to the formulae of offering (*khāthā thawājphra*) that accompany the presentation of gifts.

Despite being very sick, the aged abbot made a great effort to present himself at the most critical moment of the gift-giving ceremony. He took up his usual position in front of other monks, propped up by several large cushions, quite intent of seeing through the whole proceeding. However, the role of the leading monk for the rest of the ceremony was delegated to his deputy. The change in ritual form called for only a few adjustments, mainly the substitution of certain phrases to suit the changed situation, and the rest of the proceedings continued smoothly as if nothing had happened.

In the next part of the ceremony, the deputy abbot uttered a string of phrases constituting an intonation of a ritual formula called *jok thūnhua*, the essence of which was to ask for the merit gained to be transferred to everyone present, including spirits and angels, as well as to deceased family members and relatives of all congregants. For the benefit of celestial beings who are believed to be harbouring around the vicinity of the monastic ground, the deputy abbot intoned a formula known as *khāthā chumnumthēwadā*, inviting them to come and rejoice in the merit so made.

When the deputy abbot had finished with this incantation, the *phūnam* uttered the formula of offering (*khāthā thawājphra*), which was repeated after, phrase by phrase, by all members of the congregation, including the sponsor. The main purpose of this intonation was to formally offer the monks the gift of the yellow cloth and the accompanying items (*khryangbāuriwān*) so that merit accrued to all present, the deceased members of their families, their ancestors, their parents, and their teachers.[8]

The next part of the gift-giving ceremony involved only the sponsor and her immediate family members. Obviously, this was the moment the sponsor was waiting for. On the indication by a *sangkhārī* member she moved to the upper level of the sermon hall and sat facing the abbot and other monks. Another *sangkhārī* member then took up position on the lower level of the stepped area behind her but to her left. First he handed her a tray of the yellow cloth.[9] She presented this to the abbot, followed by a monk's bowl, an image of the Buddha, and a tray of flowers. In presenting the offerings, the items were not placed directly into the hands of the receiving monk. As the sponsor was a female, in accordance with monastic rules, she placed the items on the piece of cloth which the monk had spread out in front of him.

Several of her relatives, all women, also joined her and presented more of the gifts to the monks. When all the smaller items had been given out the deputy abbot descended to the lowest level of the stepped area to receive various items which could not be easily carried up to the raised level of the sermon hall: a kitchen sink, mats, cooking pots, flourescent lamps, and brooms. This time a male relative of the sponsor performed the presentation on her behalf. Even more items were to be presented, especially the bulkier items (the table, chairs, a large basin containing unripe bananas, crates of drinks, and so forth). These were dealt with differently again; one end of a ball of yellow cord (*sājsīn*) was secured to a leg of the table and then unwound to enclose within the boundary created the rest of the gift items. The remainder of the cord was then offered by him to the deputy abbot, symbolizing the handing over of all the items enclosed by it. The sponsor and her relatives held the trailing cord with the tips of their fingers while the ball of string was handed over to the receiving monk. Thus ended the presentation of all gift items except for the money-trees.

Ironically, the money-trees were not presented to the monks at this particular stage of the ongoing rite. Throughout the ceremony they remained at the side of the stepped area, as if totally ignored. Despite the huge capital outlay spent in their making and the apparently glamorous treatment they received in the procession, they seemed to make no item of presentation at all. Whereas great effort was involved in their making and a prominent place was given to them in the public display, as if they were *pièces de résistance* of the entire collection of gifts, during the ritual climax they were left alone. They were given due attention only afterwards when the day's ceremony was over and when most of the congregation members had gone home.

Gifts were also presented to the *phāutā* and the two *māechī*. They each received a set of white cloth and five dollars. The sponsor also presented to each of the five *sangkhārī* members a piece of men's sarong (*phāthung*, Malay: *kain pelikat*) and a piece of "shoulder" cloth (*phāploj, phākhawmā*, Malay: *kain lepas*).[10]

After all these gift items had been presented to the monks, the *phāutā*, the *māechī*, and the five *sangkhārī* members, the alms bowl which was used as the receptacle for cash donations (*anumōthanā* money) was emptied by a member of the steering committee while another member counted the total collected, which amounted to M$887.50. By right this sum belonged to the sponsor, but she decided there and then to donate it to the temple instead. The deputy monk announced her decision to the congregation.

After this, the deputy abbot rejoined other monks to chant a *suat* to bestow blessings on the crowd (*suat hajphāun*). Just before the *suat* began, another *sangkhārī* member took the ball of yellow cord, one end of which was still secured to the table leg. He wound part of the cord around a pillar at eye level and then extended the rest of the cord via other pillars around the perimeter of the lower level of the sermon hall, thereby enclosing the lay members of the congregation within a boundary formed by the cord. The other end of the cord, still in a ball, was passed in front of the seated monks and eventually placed on the far side of the last monk in the row. Each monk then took the cord and pressed it between their palms in the familiar *wāj* gesture. Soon after, the chanting began.

After the chanting, another rite followed. Despite his illness, the old abbot took over from his deputy and continued with the ceremony: a special proceeding which involved the sponsor alone. Considered to be crucial, its main objective was to enable the sponsor to express ritually her gratitude to all those present in the congregation for taking part in the day's ceremony. It included another utterance of the *truatnām* formula, transferring the merit accrued during the gift-giving ceremony to everyone present, including unseen celestial beings and spirits believed to be harbouring in the temple's vicinity. To accomplish this she repeated the formula after the abbot, phrase by phrase, whereupon the rest of the crowd followed with their own quiet recitation of a similar formula in an almost whispering tone.

This last act signified the conclusion of the day's gift-giving rite, the end of an event, meticulously planned to the very last detail, but which somehow did not quite make the *kathin* grade. The rest of the crowd started to make their exit from the sermon hall. The monks descended from the upper level, returning to their respective cubicles while the deputy abbot talked to some of the sponsor's family members.

By this time most of the congregants were on their way home, but some were to be found still lingering around various parts of the temple ground talking to one another. Still around in the sermon hall were also the five *sangkhārī* members and several others, these being the few old men and women, the temple "regulars", who usually stay a while longer to tidy up after every ceremony. The sponsor and some of the immediate members of her family also stayed behind. The gift items were taken into the storerooms of the sermon hall where they would be kept until required. This was also the time when the money-trees were at last given due attention. The banknotes were carefully removed and sorted according to denomination. At the same time the money in the monk's bowl contributed by the sponsor's guests (the *anumōthanā* money) was also sorted into stacks of a hundred dollars each and then handed over to a *sangkhārī* member who put everything into a paper bag, which he then handed over to the deputy abbot for safe keeping. The sponsor watched these informal proceedings from one corner of the sermon hall. The ceremony she had sponsored being over, she now wondered how next year's *kathin* would compare with hers.

NOTES

1. On this, Tambiah (1970, p. 160) observes that Lent is symbolic of "ascetic" Buddhism (monks in retreat, elderly full of salvation thoughts), while the *kathin* month is symbolic of "festive" Buddhism (monks emerging, the old presenting gifts, and the young participating in fairs and collective merit-making).
2. This particular monk, a Siamese of about sixty-five years old joined the monkhood for the second time. He had been ordained about twenty years before he was married. When all his children had grown up and set up families, he decided to return to the monkhood, especially after his wife had passed away. In Kelantan, monks who join the *sangha* for the second time, especially late in life, are addressed by the title of *phāu luang*. Because of their age they are not normally expected to play an active role in temple affairs, let alone take over the responsibilities already assumed by the abbot or his deputies.
3. In 1983 the temple in Bangsae had its *kathin* organized in this manner. I was given the impression by the abbot, who was also the Chief Monk of Kelantan, that the decision was apparently made in order to avoid any complications that might arise from rival factions within the temple's congregation.
4. There are four Fridays in the one-month period following the end of the *phansā* season; ideally, *kathin* ceremonies should be held on any one of these four days. Since there are at least eighteen "active" temples in the state and since ideally they have to choose from these four days, clash of events are obviously unavoidable.
5. See, for instance, Kaufman (1960, pp. 185–89), Tambiah (1970, pp. 157–60), Terwiel (1979, pp. 236–40), and Wells (1975, pp. 106–12, 173–78).
6. In Sungai Golok, a set of robes of medium quality costs more than M$100 but the same thing costs between M$80 and M$90 in Narathiwat.
7. Usually the cleaned fish is placed layer by layer in several large cooking pots, each of the layers interspaced with salt and dried rinds of a fruit the Malays call *asam gelugur* (*garcinia atroviridis*; on this vegetation, see Ridley [1922*b*, p. 173]), and steamed until cooked. The finished product will be taken to the temple kitchen where it is further prepared into various side dishes (*kabkhāw*) and served with rice to guests.
8. As mentioned by Kaufman (1960, p. 89), this is actually a reverence paid to an abstraction constituting the people who promote Buddhist learning and tradition. The exact term for this category of people is

"*upachā, khrū lāe ācān*", but I have dispensed with a literal translation fearing that it may lost its specific meaning.

9. The yellow cloth always takes precedence over other things in the sequence of giving. The cloth, like the monk's bowl, constitutes one of the eight basic necessities of the monk (*bāurikānpāet*), the cloth being the most important item in the list.

10. The "shoulder" cloth is a two-metre strip of patterned light cotton material used for various purposes: for example, as a loincloth, sash, head cover, or even as bathing cloth and towel. During rituals most people of either sex in the congregation have this piece of cloth with them as a mark of reverence. Men place the cloth, folded, on their left shoulder but women wrap it around their body from the top of the left shoulder and under the right arm like a sash. Usually one end of this strip of cloth is let loose at the front and this is spread open on the floor so that when a person prostrates (*krāb*) before a monk or a Buddha image, or during a ritual, the hands and the face rest on the cloth instead of the bare floor. See also Terwiel (1979, p. 195) and Kaufman (1960, p. 229) on the significance of this cloth as part of the ritual dress, especially on the Buddhist Sabbaths. According to Kaufman (ibid., p. 229) *phākhawmā* is a long piece of cloth worn by men as a wrap-around skirt; it is also folded and worn across the chest and one shoulder as a sign of reverence by either sex.

Chapter 7
Organizing a Temple Function

Generally, Buddhist temples in Kelantan receive no direct financial grants from the state. In order to generate the funds needed to pay for its running costs, a temple has to resort to various means to attract gifts of money and material goods from the public. During rituals on Buddhist holy days such as *āsālahabūchā*, *mākhabūchā*, *wisākhabūchā*, and *songkrān*, it is usual for people who attend the functions to make a small contribution in cash. Money is also given to the temple on other occasions such as during *kathin*, *thāut phā pā*, and ordination ceremonies. The amounts collected on these occasions may be adequate to meet the day-to-day costs of running the temple, but they are certainly not sufficient to finance extraordinary expenses.

Sometimes when temples run short of money for the construction of buildings already in progress, special merit-making ceremonies are organized and appeals sent to other Siamese villages for donations. Most villages respond by sending two or three people as representatives bearing whatever gifts of money they have collected from their fellow villagers. In 1982, for instance, when a temple in the district of Tanah Merah ran short of funds for the construction of its sermon hall, a special merit-making ceremony was organized, generating enough money to enable the temple to complete its construction by the end of the year.

Even without recourse to special merit-making occasions, the temple in Bān Klāng seldom runs into financial difficulties since monetary donations are always forthcoming from its *phuak wat*, typically from residents of the village. During my field-work it was not possible to arrive at a figure that indicates how much an individual

Siamese or Chinese household contributes annually to the temple, simply because these contributions are given in small instalments throughout the year. Apart from gifts of daily food on a roster basis, money and material goods are also given during numerous calendrical temple rites. On a single occasion a household may give between two and five dollars, plus other material items, but over the period of one year, the total sum involved, after considering the frequency of these ceremonies, is quite substantial. Nevertheless, most households do not consider this amount a strain on their family budget because it is spread out evenly throughout the year.

Visitors also contribute significantly to the temple's income. The amount contributed depends on the nature of their relationship with the temple and the monks; but at the very least the temple can expect a few dollars to be dropped into the charity box every time visitors come calling. Moreover, the majority of visitors seldom come empty-handed; the more frequent ones bring along food for the monks. This includes dry foodstuffs such as sugar, canned goods, or whatever they think appropriate for the occasion and the time of the year. During fruit seasons visitors donate the best fruit they can buy from the local market or pick from their own trees.

Contributions received from the public are used for various purposes, mainly to pay for the running expenses of the temple and for its repair and maintenance. It follows that the more money and material goods it receives, the more luxury and comfort the temple can afford. It follows too that the well-being of a temple can be measured almost instantly by making a general assessment of the physical appearance of its building, the material goods it possesses, and the facilities it offers. For instance, the fact that a temple's buildings are in a poor state of repair and maintenance says much about the kind of support it gets from the laity.

A temple well-endowed with material wealth is usually one which receives support not only from its village residents but also from outsiders. The larger the membership of its *phuak wat*, the more contributions the temple may expect. In contrast, temples which are located in remote places with difficult road access tend to be visited by fewer people and consequently receive less in terms of outside donations and help. However, this does not mean that these temples are hard-pressed for survival. In general, the residents of even the poorest villages are quite capable of providing for monks' basic needs.

Their daily food requirements are easily met by the residents of the village concerned since the number of monks to be fed is normally not large.

The image of a temple is borne by its physical appearance; hence, a huge sermon hall, large kitchen building, and sprawling dining pavilion often become the hallmarks of a temple well-endowed with ample gifts of money and material goods from its supporters. In order to have better buildings and to maintain existing ones a temple therefore has to raise money over and above the minimum required for its day-to-day running expenses. For this reason the temple lay committee often organizes special merit-making ceremonies to raise money and generate contributions of material goods from the general public. Sometimes wealthy families are solicited to become sponsors of major temple ceremonies, typically the *thāut kathin* and *thāut phā pā*. Popular temples, as noted in the last chapter, even have a waiting list of future sponsors, a considerable number of whom are Chinese.

Money collected during these occasions is saved and over the years adequate amounts are eventually accumulated to carry out renovations and necessary repairs to existing buildings. For instance, a temple in Pasir Mas district managed over a period of five years to accumulate some M$30,000 from the gifts received during its calendrical temple ceremonies and from the donations made by visitors on other occasions. This money was subsequently used to repair its ordination hall.

Dedicatory Celebrations

As already mentioned, apart from the regular donations received during the calendrical rites, huge amounts of money and material goods are given to temples during dedicatory celebrations (*ngān chalāung, ngān būchā,* Malay: *kerja ketik*).

In most cases a temple may end up collecting from this kind of function a sum of money substantially greater than the actual cost spent on the structures which are being dedicated in the celebration. For example, the total amount of money collected by the temple in Bān Klāng during a celebration to dedicate an archway and a fence in 1983 was quite substantial; it was more than sufficient to pay for the construction of the temple's new kitchen building.

Dedicatory celebrations of this nature are most common in Kelantan. At any time most temples have some kind of building project going on, its completion providing cause for celebration. Being an integral part of temple activities, such events are always looked forward to, not only by residents of the village but also by the larger temple congregation. Quite ironically, as will be seen shortly, these occasions are also eagerly anticipated by local Malays who seize the opportunity to indulge themselves in the various entertainments held within the sacred ground of the temple.

Dedicatory celebrations have a festive atmosphere, blending personal enjoyment (*khwāmsuk*) with the spiritual satisfaction of merit-making. Unlike the religious functions held on certain holy days in the Buddhist calendar (for example, *wisākhabūchā* and *mākhabūchā*), *ngān chalāung* are special occasions and usually include performances of traditional folk theatre such as *manōrā* (Malay: *menora*), *mak yong*, and shadow-puppet shows. Other forms of entertainment include *ramwong*[1] and lately the staging of open-air concerts in which professional troupes of singers and dancers from Thailand perform Broadway-style musical reviews which the Siamese refer to as *phuak dontrī*. Although the more traditional kind of entertainments such as *manōrā* and *mak yong* is becoming less frequent, because there are now fewer theatrical groups, many temples still include them in their programmes. Other entertainment on these special festive occasions includes the raffling of expensive prizes and games of chance, the proceeds of which go to the temple's coffers.

Temple celebrations of the festive kind (*kān mahāurasob*) carry special meaning for the Siamese as a minority group. The temple is virtually the only locale where they may organize these performances in relative freedom, without having to consider the sensitivities of their Malay neighbours and various bureaucratic regulations regarding entertainments and gaming activity. However, this does not mean that Malays are excluded entirely from temple fairs and celebrations. Indeed, a considerable number of local Malays are attracted by the entertainment provided. In fact, it has always been the tradition that during such celebrations Malays from surrounding villages form a significant part of the audience, although no Malays are known to participate in merit-making ceremonies or other religiously oriented activities. Where tickets are sold, the presence of

Malays, who come in considerable numbers from various villages in the district, helps to increase the gate. However, the fact that these entertainments are taking place within the temple compound reminds the Malays that they are merely spectators whose freedom of access to Siamese territory is well tolerated.

Although Malays are admitted into the temple ground during these dedicatory celebrations, their presence is appropriate only at certain times. Malays go to the temple essentially to watch the entertainment, so it is only during the evening, when the shows start, that they are seen mingling with the Siamese and Chinese crowd. At other times during the course of the celebration, Malays are not to be seen, except for one or two who have close friends in the village. They are also to refrain from making a tour of religiously significant parts of the temple such as the ordination and sermon halls. Although food is served to the public, Malays are not expected to eat at the temple kitchen.[2] Partly for this reason, the organizing committee of the temple sets up stalls catering for Malay customers, selling bottled drinks and a limited variety of food: mainly plastic-wrapped snacks brought from outside the village, but seldom cooked food prepared by the Siamese on the spot.[3]

Dedicatory celebrations also bring together Siamese from all over Kelantan and many parts of southern Thailand. Invitations are extended to as many people as possible. This the temple committee does by word of mouth, particularly while attending temple functions held at other places, and also through specially printed leaflets (*batchōen*), which are printed in Thai, Malay, and sometimes Chinese.

The response to these appeals is almost spontaneous. Without fail, members of the laity and monks from these villages make a point of sending at least one or two persons as representatives, particularly if such functions are held in far-away places and if mass transportation proves to be a major problem. From villages more accessible by good road, busloads of people arrive to take part in the celebration. Some villages are known to send to the host village an advance party of monks, men, and women to help with preparations for the celebration. Nor is it uncommon to see monks from distant places, including Thailand, arriving two or three days ahead of the day of celebration to give whatever assistance they can or to provide advice on matters concerning the organization of the function.

Sometimes, for various reasons those from distant villages may not be able to attend the celebrations in person, but this does not mean that they are denied the opportunity of making merit. They may still do so by giving "absentee contributions" ranging from two to five dollars or more through fellow villagers who can make it to the function. Normally at least one or two persons from every Siamese village in the Kelantan region will attend any such ceremony, often the *sangkhārī* members of these settlements.

Apart from the Siamese, Chinese from towns and other Chinese settlements in the state are also invited. Kinship ties between these Chinese and the residents of Bān Klāng ensure that the former are invited to participate in merit-making ceremonies and other celebrations at the temple. Influential Chinese, particularly those who operate various businesses in town and have a wide range of social contacts, are often invited to sit on the temple working committees specially set up to organize such celebrations.[4] Their reason for doing so is pragmatic: the usual rule is that it is always good politics to include the Chinese because many of the building projects, which are the focus of these celebrations in the first place, are a result mainly of the money that they contributed. In addition, the temples also receive other indirect benefits from many Chinese business establishments in Kelantan. For instance, building materials are bought, usually at hefty discounts, from Chinese shops whose owners are known to the temple and the monastic community.

These occasions therefore also generate a sense of pride among the Chinese since their patronage is recognized and acknowledged in various ways, including the writing of the names of contributors in the appropriate place on the structures erected. For instance, the base of the archway at the main entrance of Bān Klāng's temple carries two plaques bearing the names of those who contributed towards the cost of its construction; all but one are Chinese. It is common for space to be reserved in this way on the façade of many buildings and monastic structures to record the names of donors and sometimes the amount they contributed as well.

Hitherto the most prestigious building project (and perhaps the most expensive) ever undertaken by a Siamese temple in Kelantan was the construction of a reclining image of the Buddha, 42 metres long and 10 metres high, said to be the biggest of its kind in the country. This ambitious project belongs to a temple located in Tumpat district. The abbot of this temple is not only one of the more

outgoing monks in Kelantan but also one of the two who are ethnically Chinese.

The construction of the statue started in 1973 and was completed
in 1983, costing around M$160,000. The donors included a large
proportion of the members of its congregation, Buddhists elsewhere in the state, and visitors from various parts of Malaysia and
southern Thailand. Souvenir publications in the form of booklets
distributed to guests during the dedicatory celebration of the image
contain, not surprisingly, quite a number of advertisements for
Chinese business concerns, testifying to the support the temple is
getting from the Chinese. A giant overhead shelter for the reclining
statue estimated to cost M$400,000 had already been planned, and
the dedicatory celebration in 1983 raised a large sum of money to
initiate this project. In 1980 the Supreme Patriarch of Thailand
(*Phrasangkharāt*) visited the temple to bless the image. The statue has
now become one of Kelantan's main tourist attractions, and most
tours operators are expected to include in their package a trip to this
temple, where souvenirs are sold by villagers on behalf of the temple.

Dedicatory Celebration at the Temple in Bān Klāng

Nearly every temple has an archway which marks the main entrance
to the monastic grounds. This structure usually bears a statue or a
painted image of the Buddha and bas-relief images depicting characters of Indic origin, typically those of the god Indra (*Phra In*). The
archway also bears the temple's name, usually written on a decorative
top panel, in Thai. In addition to Thai, other languages are often
used, including Malay, Chinese, and English.

The archway that spans the main entrance of the temple in Bān
Klāng was a gift from a group of residents of the village, joint owners
of one of the two tobacco-curing companies of the village. The
original estimate of costs to build the structure was around M$15,000,
but when it was finally completed in early 1983 the actual sum
expended came close to M$25,000. For the construction, Siamese
craftsmen of the village were hired while resident monks of the
temple helped in whatever way they could. Despite the fact that the
costs of construction were fully borne by the Chinese, the design and
the style of the archway remain distinctively Siamese. However, the
names of the donors were inscribed in romanized spelling on the two

plaques fixed to the base panels of the archway. This is the only indication that the structure was a Chinese gift.

Although the construction of the archway and the temple fence was completed in early 1983, the dedicatory celebration did not take place until May, about five months later. This delay was deliberate, calculated to take into account the tobacco-growing season, which normally ends in April. Whereas people were too preoccupied with work in the fields during the planting season, to hold the celebration after the harvest was a perfect timing, because most households in the village have a good reserve of cash, this being the proceeds from the sale of tobacco.

Moreover, it was simply not practical to hold a large-scale temple celebration during the growing season, since the areas immediately surrounding the temple are heavily planted with tobacco. To organize it during the season would threaten valuable crops caused by the attending crowd trampling upon the tobacco plants. For the ceremony extra space was also needed for parking motor cars, motor cycles, and bicycles, and after the harvest the bare tobacco fields served this purpose well. At the same time a number of Malay traders also wished to take the opportunity to sell their wares outside the temple gate in an open-air night bazaar (*pasar malam*), during which a wide range of items were offered for sale, including cooked food, drinks, clothing, toys, kitchenware, and household goods. These vendors too needed clear space to do so. In short, in view of all these considerations, it appears that the cycle of the growing season now determines the date of a major temple celebration.

Prior to most temple celebrations invitation circulars (*batchōen*) are widely distributed to Siamese villages in Kelantan and southern Thailand. Judging by the circulars printed for the celebration at Bān Klāng's temple, the working committee looked very impressive indeed. Heading this distinguished committee was the Chief Monk of Kelantan (*caw khana rat*) as the honourable sponsor (*phū upatham*). Also included were two high-ranking district head monks (*caw khana amphōe*), one from from Pasir Mas (in Kelantan) and the other from Sungai Padi (in Thailand). Also on the list was a monk of a temple in Nikhom Waeng, a land settlement in Narathiwat province of southern Thailand, where some of its pioneers originated from Bān Klāng.

Those who represented the laity on the grand committee consisted of two members of the temple's *sangkhārī*. Also included were influential Chinese residents of the village, including the headman. All told, there were nine people on the list who represented the laity, five Chinese and four Siamese.

An interesting point about this committee is that those who represented the *sangha* were all Siamese, while those who represented the laity were either Chinese or Siamese. One of the Chinese who represented the laity was not even a resident of Bān Klāng but was nevertheless included in the committee for pragmatic reasons: he was an executive member of the local branch of the Malaysian Chinese Association (MCA), a major political party in the government coalition. His greatest contribution to the success of the celebration was arranging for special immigration permit for the musical troupe from Thailand. Had it not been for his contact with the local bureaucracy the permit would not have been so easily obtained. In fact, MCA party members have been instrumental in many other respects as well, as in helping to iron out some of the problems normally encountered whenever functions of such a grand scale are organized. The task of getting official permission for the performance and for setting up stalls during the celebration was also left to MCA members. As the celebration involved a large gathering of different ethnic communities, drunkenness and fights could not be ruled out. Generally, the local authorities are cautious about giving permission unless some respected community member provides an assurance that unruly behaviour will not occur. On this occasion the MCA executive members and the headman both gave their word that adequate crowd control would be provided by the organizing committee. The help rendered by the MCA members did not go unrewarded. A decorative archway — a temporary structure to be displayed only for the duration of the celebration — bearing the party's name was erected across the approach road to the temple. This imposing structure served to remind visitors attending the temple function of the role played by MCA party members.

The inclusion of Chinese residents of Bān Klāng in the organizing committee is not unusual when temple celebrations are organized on a large scale. They usually have good contacts with members of the Chinese business community in Kelantan's major towns, and Chinese companies respond very generously if approached to support temple celebrations. For instance, a vehicle dealer in Kota Bharu contributed three brand-new motor cycles as prizes in a raffle held in conjunction with the performance of a musical troupe from Thailand. Another trading company that distributes petroleum products gave a substantial cash donation during the celebration. In return, banners advertising both companies' products were allowed to be hung over the entrance leading to the place where the concert was held and at the main gate of the temple.

Initial preparations for the celebration began about two months ahead, when women washed and sorted kitchenware retrieved from the storerooms while men attended to whatever repairs were necessary around the temple. Unoccupied living quarters had their broken floor boards replaced, a leaking roof was fixed, new coats of paint were applied to the interior and exterior walls of the sermon hall, and the temple compound was cleared of all rubbish. Finishing touches were given to the archway itself, the focus of the celebration. In its overall appearance the entire temple was given a new lease of life.

Close to one week prior to the date of the celebration, the backyard section of the temple compound was fenced off to provide an enclosed area for the performance of the musical troupe from Thailand. Six stalls were built inside this enclosure from which food and drinks were sold to the crowd attending the concert. One of these stalls offered games of chance of the kind generally seen at fairs.

An important part of organizing temple celebrations is the preparation of cooked food to feed the large number of participants. In Kelantan it is customary for both guests and residents of the village hosting a function to eat at the temple during the course of the celebration. Food and drinks are normally served at specially built shelters or in the temple kitchens if they are spacious enough. A kitchen committee sees to this and arriving guests are shown to these places where they are properly attended to. This committee is appointed by the temple steering committee (*sangkhārī*), but in the normal course of events many more people are actually involved, especially women volunteers who come to help prepare and serve food to guests.

The custom of feeding guests is especially important in rural villages where there are not many eating shops. Even if there are some, these shops are unlikely to have the capacity to cater for the large number of people. Accordingly, the temple usually provides enough food for all who care to eat, even during smaller religious rites. Although during minor ceremonies the food brought along is intended for the monks, there is usually enough food to be shared by all attending. Generally, outsiders expect to be provided with at least the mid-day meal whenever they attend temple functions.

The reason for providing food to members of the congregation who attend was explained by one of the *sangkhārī* members of Bān Klāng's temple: since most people who come to the temple give a donation of some sort, usually money, it is appropriate that the temple should reciprocate accordingly; at least the mid-day meals should be on the house. This arrangement also grows out of consideration for people who may arrive at the temple from distant places quite famished after the journey. The same *sangkhārī* member also explained that people are willing to contribute generously if they are served ample food and refreshments. Furthermore, part of the money used to purchase the provisions had been previously contributed by visitors.

Seeing that guests are properly fed is one of the major concerns of the temple organizing committee. Temples which do not serve adequate food to their guests normally become the subject of gossip. To ensure that cooked food is plentiful, the committee in charge normally over-estimate the number of guests arriving, the standing policy being to prepare more food than is actually required. Extra stores of provisions, such as rice and other items, are kept as a contingency. To run short of food is very embarrassing to the host committee and reflects badly on the temple that organizes the function.

The large number of people attending a temple function means that special arrangements have to be made with regard to the kinds of food served and the quantities involved. It also means that the temple must have adequate facilities to prepare and serve food to the guests. This explains why nearly every temple endeavours to have a large kitchen complex, complete with all sorts of cooking and eating utensils, and a dining hall spacious enough to cater for a capacity crowd.

For large temple functions the choice of the menu falls upon food that is easy to prepare in bulk and which keeps quite easily for days, requiring no elaborate method of storage. The most common food served at major temple functions is either *khāwjam* (Malay: *nasi kerabu*) or *khanomcīn* (Malay: *laksa*).[5] Both are simple to prepare and do not require elaborate and numerous side dishes. Ordinary white rice, in contrast, normally requires two or three kinds of side dishes and this entails far more work. These preferred foods can be prepared in bulk and by nature can keep for the whole day or even until the next day without having to be specially stored. In general, the food served at temple functions need not be sumptuous; what matters is that it should be filling. No fancy foods or delicacies are prepared, except those served to monks and some selected guests.[6]

In order to feed the large number of people attending the celebration at Bān Klāng's temple, a work-force consisting of seventy-four men and women was formed and assigned the responsibility of preparing and serving food to the guests.[7] These people, representing various households of the village, were divided into three groups, each taking turns to carry out its responsibility.

On the first three days of the celebration, *khāwjam* was served as the main meal. The food bill was estimated to be around M$4,000. Some of the supplies consisting of uncooked rice, fresh vegetables, coconut, sugar, and canned milk were contributed by various households of the village and also by outsiders. Nevertheless, six extra sacks of rice of about 100 kilogrammes each were bought, plus another sack of sugar as a contingency measure. Most of the stock was consumed by the end of the fourth day of the celebration.

The dedicatory celebration (*ngān chalāung*) of 1983 was a notable event in Bān Klāng because there had been no undertaking like it since the one held in 1976. Organized to dedicate the building that houses a replica of the Buddha's footprint relic (*phraphutthabāt camlāung*),[8] the 1976 celebration was a four-day affair in which people from other villages also took part. There were also performances of *ramwong* and shadow-puppet shows, and a special sermon (*thētsanā*) was delivered by the Chief Monk of Kelantan.

The 1983 dedicatory celebration was planned to take place also for four consecutive days, 19 to 22 May. On the first day of the celebration (*wan rōem ngān*), delegations of monks representing various temples in Kelantan and southern Thailand took part in the presentation ceremony, headed by the Chief Monk of Kelantan. Although the day's ceremony was very brief, starting at about nine o'clock in the morning, it was most impressive and colourful. A special platform had been erected inside the temple compound next to the archway, the main reason for the celebration, to seat nine monks who represented various temples of Kelantan and southern Thailand. The ceremony began with the Chief Monk reading a short speech accepting the gift of the archway and the fence on behalf of the state's *sangha*. Then he cut the ribbon that was stretched across the archway. As soon as this was done, the nine monks read a chant (*suat cayantō*), while a group of musicians that normally takes the lead in processions around the temple during other major merit-making ceremonies played their instruments. Another orchestra, consisting of what remained of the village's *manōrā* group, played music in a distinctive style of its own. The temple drums and bells were also sounded at this moment. The sounds of the chanting monks, the two orchestras, the drums, and bells, almost indescribable in their usual combinations, marked the climax of the morning's ceremony. When all this had finished, about fifty helium-filled coloured balloons were released into the air, attached to a cloth banner about 3 metres long on which was inscribed in Thai and Malay the date of the auspicious occasion.[9]

At about 10.30 a.m. three men were ordained as novices. One candidate was a Siamese resident of Bān Klāng, the other two were Chinese from two small towns in the district. Later in the afternoon they were ordained as monks in the "token" manner (*buat bon*); their stay in the *sangha* lasted for only three days. In Kelantan people are known to organize ordination ceremonies, mainly of the "token" kind, whenever large functions are held at the temple in order to capitalize on occasions when large numbers of people are present.

At about four o'clock in the afternoon, the residents of Bān Klāng formed a procession bearing money-trees. The households in the village were previously divided into groups of eight to ten, each group responsible for making a money-tree to be presented to the temple. Every household in the group contributed between twenty and fifty dollars towards the making of a tree. Two of the money-trees presented that day deserve special mention. While most trees were made in the customary way from banana trunks and strips of bamboo fastened with metal wires and decorated with coloured paper ribbons, these two trees were rather innovative, being symbolic of what had become a major occupation of Bān Klāng. Two tobacco trees — replanted, root and all, in two tin cans, their leaves stapled with banknotes and decorated with artificial flowers and coloured ribbons — were presented by a group of households whose members have a major controlling interest in the tobacco companies of the village.

The procession did not involve the entire village, but represent-atives of most households were present. It started at the junction of the main road and the approach road of the temple and resembled that conducted during the *kathin* ceremony (already described in Chapter 6). It was also led by a group of young people playing music on traditional percussion instruments consisting of four long drums, two short drums, cymbals, and two pieces of wood clapping against each other. This was the same group that had previously played at the presentation ceremony in the morning. As usual, the procession went round the ordination hall three times before going into the sermon hall for the final rite of presentation.

The people of Bān Klāng chose to parade their money-trees on the first day of the celebration because on the subsequent three days they would be preoccupied with various kinds of work. Most had been assigned duties such as cooking, serving food and drinks to guests, and washing plates and utensils. Their ritual procession had to take place before the grand occasion of merit-making the next day, when laypersons and members of the clergy from other villages and temples would arrive with their contributions of money-trees and other gift items. In one sense, the procession of money-trees on the first day symbolized the collective effort of the residents of Bān Klāng; in contrast, the offering of money-trees by outsiders on the second day symbolized the involvement of other members of the congregation and Buddhists from elsewhere in the state in the temple's projects and affairs.

On the second day of the celebration people from other Siamese villages arrived to take part in the merit-making ceremony, bringing along their money-trees and other gift items. Every time groups of people arrived by cars or chartered buses they were met at the main road by the temple's band of musicians, which led them around the ordination hall three times before bringing them into the sermon hall. There the waiting *sangkhārī* members received the delegations. A short rite of the presentation of gifts to the monks took place, a pro-cedure repeated by every new group arriving at the temple. At least one of the *sangkhārī* members was present at all times to receive these delegations. Immediately after all the gifts were presented to the temple the guests were shown to the dining sheds where the main meal was served. This continued for the whole day until late in the afternoon, when the last delegation would have arrived.

Most of those who had eaten did not go home immediately but stayed on within the temple compound to meet other people, friends, and relatives. The younger ones looked forward to the evening's entertainment programme, while the elderly remained in the sermon hall following closely whatever rites were going on inside. Many of the guests spent the night at the temple. Some slept in vacant monks' quarters, others in the buildings of the second temple. Yet others were invited to spend the night with relatives and friends at their homes in the lay residential quarters of Bān Klāng.

The second day of the celebration was of great significance. Bān Klāng became the focal point for the gathering of delegations of people and monks representing various Siamese villages in the region. Nearly all Kelantan Siamese settlements and other satellites elsewhere were represented at this stage of the celebration. This was also the occasion when the rural Chinese of Kelantan and some of their urban counterparts who also supported Buddhist temples turned up to attend the function.

On the third day of the celebration a procession was organized outside the temple gate similar to the one held on the first day, only this time a careful selection was made of various gift items and money-trees accumulated during the last two days. This selection was supposed to represent the collection of gifts contributed by residents of Bān Klāng as a community, by outsiders as members of the congregation, and by other Siamese settlements and temples as an expression of their membership of the wider Buddhist population in the area. Involving more people than those previously held, the parade bearing these gifts was a manifestation of the total Buddhist population of Kelantan. This procession ended with the rite of presentation (*thawāj khryangthān*), which was similar to that held on the previous two days except that a larger number of gifts and money-trees were involved.

On the last day of the celebration there was a rite of giving of food to the monks (*sajbāt; thakbāt*) just before they took their noon meal. By this time most of the guests had gone home, leaving only the few who had stayed behind to help tidy up the temple area after nearly four days of celebration and merit-making. By the afternoon of the same day the festive atmosphere had abated almost completely. The musical troupe from Thailand had packed up and returned home.

Although the temple looked quite deserted, there were still some activity in the sermon hall. The various gifts donated by other temples and guests were unpacked and placed in the storerooms of the sermon hall by the *sangkhārī* members with the help of some of the laity who had stayed behind. The money-trees, which had also been kept in the storerooms over the previous three days, were brought out. A number of these trees were entrusted to a group of men and women who unfastened the banknotes, sorted them according to denominations, and recounted them before handing them over to one of the *sangkhārī* members, who then verified the amount. The bundle of banknotes was later given to the deputy abbot for safe keeping. He recorded the amount and the names of the contributors in a small notebook that he kept with him all the time.

The money-trees were not counted all at once, nor was the same group of laity involved in the counting. Throughout the afternoon four or five trees were removed at a time from the storerooms and assigned to one group of laity. When all the banknotes on these trees had been counted, another fresh group of laity would take over the assignment involving another set of trees. By late afternoon a considerable number of trees had been counted, with only a few still remaining in the storerooms. Although the counting was done openly in the sermon hall, at this stage nobody really knew the exact value of the money collected, partly because of the constant replacement of people involved in the counting and partly because the trees were not brought out and counted all at once. The only person who could give the right figure was the deputy abbot. Even the *sangkhārī* members could not work out the final tally accurately.

Rotating the people to do the counting was mainly for the sake of security in view of the large amount of money involved. About one hundred trees were donated with an estimated value of between M$300 and M$500 each, which works out to a total of between M$30,000 and M$40,000. Again, no one was really sure of the exact number of trees donated to the temple since most of them were whisked away into the storeroom by attending *sangkhārī* members as soon as they were ritually presented by the groups bearing them. Only a token number of trees were displayed on the stepped area of the sermon hall at any time throughout the course of the celebration; the rest were kept in the storerooms under tight security.

During the second, third, and fourth nights of the celebration a musical troupe from Thailand (*dontrī*) performed in the enclosed area behind the ordination hall. As this open-air concert was also organized to raise money for the temple, entrance fees were charged. Tickets were sold at M$8 per adult and M$5 for children. Although a capacity audience turned up on the first night, the attendance on the other two nights was poor. This was made worse by a power failure on these two consecutive nights. Those attending were quite frustrated by the interruption and although the power was eventually restored others who had planned to see the show on the third night, fearing another power failure, changed their minds. As overhead cables supplying electricity to Bān Klāng passed through Malay villages, rumours were rife that the failure was the outcome of sabotage by their Malay neighbours who short-circuited the power lines, although there was no concrete proof of this. Furthermore, power failures are quite common in rural Kelantan, sometimes lasting for days on end, hitting not only Siamese villages, but the whole district as well.

The takings for the first night amounted to about M$8,000 and out of this M$3,000 was paid to the troupe. The takings from the following two nights were much less. Because of the poor turn-out of the audience, particularly on the third night, the management of the troupe therefore decided not to charge performance fees for the last night and assigned all receipts to the temple.

The celebration associated with the dedication of Bān Klāng's new archway and fence took place in a festive atmosphere typical of similar functions held in other temples in Kelantan. Despite the large Chinese attendance and the substantial Chinese donations of money to the temple, the grand occasion was essentially a Siamese affair, not only in spirit but also in form and content. The proceedings of the four-day ceremony were conducted in a truly Siamese temple tradition, despite the fact that the archway was built almost entirely with Chinese money.

The circulars announcing the celebration are revealing in this respect. They were printed in Thai on one side and Malay on the other. One might have expected that, since about half of the village's population is Chinese, the circulars would have also been printed in the Chinese script. However, it appears that the *sangkhārī* members did not consider doing so, partly because of their assumption that many of the rural Chinese could hardly read the Chinese language.

This explanation given looks rather inadequate; the circular would be more rewarding to the temple if it were to be addressed to the wider Chinese society, which includes town-dwelling and mainstream Chinese from whom monetary and material support could also be expected. For this reason and considering the fact that many socially and politically prominent Chinese (including the MCA members) also sat on the organizing committee, the non-usage of Chinese in the circular makes the explanation given by the *sangkhārī* far from convincing.

Another intriguing feature of the invitation circulars is the usage of a language style of some sophistication known to those who have received some degree of monastic and formal Thai education. Elegant terminologies normally found in monastic writing were deliberately incorporated in the Thai version of the *batchōen*. In contrast, the language of the Malay translation was almost colloquial in style and seemed to have been meant for the majority of the Chinese members of the congregation whose command of formal Malay was limited.

The Thai version of the circular announced that the coming event was to be "a celebration according to the popular tradition of the Thai people".[10] However, translated with a slightly different gloss into the Malay version, the same phrase was rendered as "a celebration … according to the traditions of the Buddhist people",[11] a perhaps deliberate mis-translation obviously to accommodate, and to avoid slighting, Chinese supporters of the temple. There could also be another reason for the mis-translation; in the context of Thailand and the Thai nation-state the term "Thai" is synonymous to "Buddhist".

Although the invitation circular contained an impressive array of people who made up the organizing committee, some of these names were purposely included in order to give the occasion an air of authority and grandeur. Thus the Chief Monk of Kelantan was included as a matter of symbolic significance because ecclesiastical affairs, including temple celebrations, rightfully come under his jurisdiction.[12] Likewise, the inclusion of high-ranking monks from Thailand (such as the *caw khana amphōe* of Sungai Padi) and the monk from the *nikhom* settlement gave the occasion an authentic Thai atmosphere. In an equally pragmatic way, some Chinese were also drawn into the organizing committee; the headman of the village, who was also a Chinese, was included in the committee perhaps because of the official position he held.[13] Such was also the case with the MCA members and influential Chinese entrepreneurs of the village.

On the whole, one is tempted to conclude that the impressive array of names listed in the *batchōen* was a mere formality, a symbolic declaration, while the hard work of organizing the celebration and other co-ordinating responsibilities in fact fell on the deputy abbot, the monks, members of the *sangkhārī*, and some of the village elders forming the élite group that looked after temple affairs. In other words, it was the closed group of the village's religious élite, comprising mainly Siamese, that was really involved in organizing the celebration. Despite this, the celebration went well because the working committee was able to rally support and co-operation not only from the residents of the village but also from members of the larger congregation of the temple.

It is also during such occasions that one can observe the varying levels of Chinese participation in temple affairs. For instance, a Chinese businessman from Kota Bharu who had donated a generous sum of money was at the temple during the second day of the celebration but did not join the worshippers in the sermon hall. He remained at the pavilion with other Chinese, some of them his business colleagues who, like himself, were attracted to temple celebrations but were quite reluctant to be involved in the rituals going on inside. Although he and his friends appeared to be quite aloof, taking no active part in the rituals, their contributions were nevertheless expressive of their support of the temple.

Likewise a number of Chinese from various townships of Kelantan and even from other states made day trips to the temple during the celebration but, despite the large donations they were known to have made, did not take any active part in the rituals. Yet their very presence was of great significance because it expressed the kind of support the temple enjoys from the Chinese public. There were also a number of town-dwelling Chinese who came to the celebration mainly out of curiosity generated perhaps by the publicity given to such events, the news of which tend to circulate very widely among the local Chinese population.

Of course, some Chinese visitors were more involved in the ritual than others. For instance, a typical Chinese family from one of the townships in Kelantan spent the whole day at the temple but, again, only some elderly members of the family, mainly women, entered the sermon hall to join other worshippers. Meanwhile, the husband, the young son, and the grandchildren waited outside the building in one of the empty monks' quarters, keeping themselves busy as observers rather than as active participants.

As already seen, Bān Klāng temple seldom runs short of money and material support. Its congregation comprising both residents of the village and outsiders who are either Chinese or Siamese continuously provides for its needs. The major difference between Chinese and Siamese supporters of the temple lies in the fact that while the former are generous in giving money and material support, the latter are more involved in the actual running of temple affairs. The more permanent members of the clergy and the people who constitute the religious élite of the village are always predominantly Siamese. As the case of Bān Klāng's celebration illustrates, Chinese involvement is limited in the actual organization of the occasion, let alone in the intricacies of temple rituals, even though their contributions of money to the institution far exceed what the Siamese themselves can provide.

A final remark should be made concerning the Chinese owners of the tobacco company who jointly donated the archway. One might have expected them to be given special recognition, at least during the brief event over which the Chief Monk of the state presided. After all, if not for their money the celebration would not have been held at all. Yet their importance was overshadowed by the nine monks who were seated on a specially erected dais, and by the Chief Monk who represented the state *sangha*. Although huge sums of money from the Chinese were involved, the Chinese never really exerted any decisive influence on the actual running of the function. In fact, as the celebration unfolded, it became clear that the four-day affair was essentially Siamese both in content and in form.

NOTES

1. In central Thai dialect the term means some sort of dance, but in Kelantan, the term is more applicable to a group of young (and not-so-young) girls who dance with members of the audience by ticket. A special platform is built within the temple compound for this purpose. Apparently, it is also very popular with the Malay audience; hence the

large number of Malay males present whenever *ramwong* performances are staged.

2. One main reason for this is their taboo against pork. For more details on Malay avoidance of commensality at temples as well as at Siamese and Chinese houses, see the Appendix.

3. Malay petty traders often take advantage of temple celebrations to sell cooked food outside the temple compound on the nights that entertainments are held because of the assured patronage they get from Malays attending the show.

4. This working committee is not to be confused with the permanent steering committee of the temple, the *sangkhārī*.

5. *Khāwjam* or *nasi kerabu* consists of plain white rice mixed with finely chopped vegetables and herbs, dry-fried grated coconut flavoured with fish floss, and fish sauce (*nāmplā*). Sometimes thick gravy made from coconut milk and chilli goes with it. There may also be pieces of fried chicken or fish served but these last two items are optional. *Khanomcīn* or *laksa* consists of thick rice noodles served with coconut-milk gravy, flavoured with fish and relished with chopped herbs and vegetables. Since the noodles, bought in bulk from the local market or ordered directly from Thailand, are already cooked one need only prepare the accompanying gravy and vegetable relishes.

6. They are mostly eminent Chinese businessmen who are singled out by the reception committee and entertained separately. Many of them are current employers of residents who work in the town where these Chinese come from.

7. This figure was given by one the *sangkhārī* members, but I suspect more people were actually involved, especially when others not originally on the list, men and women volunteers from distant villages, turned up to help when the celebration started. I have not been able to determine how many of this number involved were Chinese and Siamese, but the man heading this work-force, who also kept account of the money used to purchase the food was Siamese. Although not a member of the *sangkhārī*, he was one of those who rightly belonged to the religious élite of the village.

8. Structure no. 10 in Figure 4.1.

9. Incidently, a note was also written, in Malay, to the effect that if the banner were to be found and returned to the temple, a reward awaited the finder. However, nothing has been heard of it ever since.

10. *Kān chalāung tām praphēnī nijom khāung khon thaj.*

11. *Perayaan . . . mengikut adat resam kaum Buddha.*

12. The Chief Monk himself arrived at the temple on the first day of the celebration, in time for the opening ceremony of the archway and the fence, but left soon after the mid-day meal.
13. In fact, the headman himself was not deeply involved in the rites that took place during the four-day celebration. He chose to make brief appearances occasionally at the temple, but certainly not during critical moments of the celebration. Thus during the rite of gift-offering on the third day, the headman, perhaps preoccupied with other things, was not to be seen anywhere around the temple, although his father, who was the only Chinese *sangkhārī*, was there.

Chapter 8
Buddhism and the Meaning of Siamese Ethnicity

The main concern of this study has been with Theravāda Buddhism as it is practised in a village in Kelantan. This study serves to illustrate that despite the overwhelmingly Malay and Muslim nature of Kelantanese rural society, Buddhism thrives as a minority religion, in particular among the Siamese. It is through Buddhism that the Siamese have been able to maintain their distinctiveness as an ethnic group *vis-à-vis* both Malays and other ethnic groups, including the Chinese.

The village of study, Bān Klāng, is by no means exclusively Siamese in ethnic composition. About half of its population is Chinese, yet all who live in the settlement regard themselves as members of a community which is culturally Siamese in many ways. This characteristic is attributable to the existence in the village of a Siamese Buddhist temple together with its monastic residents, as well as to the fact that the Chinese residents of the village are also involved in various temple-based social and religious activities.

This study has also emphasized the fact that there are fundamental differences between Siamese and Chinese Buddhists, reflected in their varying levels of commitment and adherence to the Buddhist religion. The membership of the "religious élite" illustrates the exclusiveness which ensures continuing Siamese dominance in the social and religious organization of Theravāda Buddhism in Kelantan. While both Chinese and Siamese are Buddhists, the latter are more involved in the religion. While Chinese support is undoubtedly important for the continued maintenance of the temple and its clergy, it is the Siamese who are more involved in providing the personnel to staff the institution on a permanent basis. Hence, the membership of the religious élite is almost exclusively Siamese, and control of the organization of the Buddhist religion at both village and regional levels is vested in Siamese hands.

The temple of Bān Klāng provides services not only to residents of this village but also to the Buddhist population of other outlying areas where many rural Chinese and pockets of Siamese live in settlements lacking temples of their own. As for the rural Chinese, despite being congregation members of the temple, they continue to engage in some distinctively Chinese religious practices, which differentiate them from Siamese Buddhists. The Bān Klāng temple meanwhile is part of a regional religious network which covers Kelantan, southern Thailand, and northern Terengganu which, in terms of the Buddhist ecclesiastical hierarchy, may be considered an extension of the Thai *sangha*. The network binds together the Buddhists of Kelantan with those of other places in the region.

The participation of the rural Chinese in temple rituals and ceremonies also serves to underwrite their sense of belonging and identity. For instance, involvement in temple-based activities places the Chinese residents of Bān Klāng in the same community as the Siamese. Together with other rural Chinese who are not residents of Bān Klāng, they share with the Siamese similar religious commitments from which a kind of social and cultural alliance develops between the two ethnic groups. In a predominantly Malay society, rural Chinese, who like the Siamese are also a minority group, choose to align themselves with similar groups. Their association with the Siamese exemplifies the case of one minority identifying with another when confronted with perceived threats, even if only imaginary, from — or simply the overwhelming cultural presence of — a dominant majority.

Rural Chinese prefer alliance with the Siamese to alliance with the Malays because of the good social relationships, mainly in the form of kinship ties dating back several decades, that link the Siamese and the rural Chinese. In addition, the familiarity of earlier generations of rural Chinese with the Buddhist religion, even though not of the Theravāda type, has facilitated such an identification. Moreover, Chinese religion is very accommodative, and the familiarity of the first Chinese migrants with Buddhism while in China made Siamese Buddhism more attractive than, say, Hinduism or Islam. Most important, identification with the Siamese through Buddhism does not entail any loss of Chinese ethnic identity. This contrasts with the adoption of Islam by any non-Malay group; to become a Muslim in the Malaysian and Kelantanese context means to forgo one's ethnic identity; one has to become Malay at the same time. Unlike conversion to Islam, adherence to Theravāda Buddhism does not entail "a confession of faith" (Tobias 1977, p. 313) and therefore requires no renunciation of any previous religious affiliation. Despite being Buddhists, the rural Chinese of Kelantan may identify themselves with the mainstream Chinese of Malaysia, which the Siamese could not do. At the same time, identification with the Theravāda Buddhist tradition enables the rural Chinese of Kelantan to differentiate themselves from the mainstream Chinese. In relation to the ethnic categories of national level politics, they are primarily Chinese; but at the level of face-to-face interaction in Kelantan, they are Buddhists, with a status resembling and merging with that of the Siamese. In this way, in a context of overwhelming Malay cultural and political dominance, they align themselves with a locally protected and unthreatening minority group, thereby distancing, detaching, and disassociating themselves from a larger minority group seen at the national level as powerful and threatening.

There is also another significant distinction between Chinese Buddhists and Siamese Buddhists. The rural Chinese, despite being Buddhists, also practise religious beliefs that are essentially part of general Chinese religion, which though alien are tolerated by the Siamese. Hence, it is not uncommon for some practices associated with Chinese religion to "infiltrate" Siamese temples. There is now a growing trend in some temples to accommodate the religious demand exerted by the Chinese; Chinese deities are given appropriate places in the temple's compound although they may not necessarily occupy the most strategic locations in terms of Buddhist ritual context. On the other hand, the rural Chinese too accommodate themselves to some Siamese cultural and religious practices. A case in point is ordination, which for the Siamese is not only the cultural hallmark of being a Siamese but also of being a devout Buddhist and foremost in the religious act of renunciation. The majority of Chinese monks pass through ordination of the "token" type, since ordination for a prolonged period is by no means typical Chinese cultural behaviour. In so far as renunciation is concerned, the Chinese, to use Wijeyewardene's term, have "misunderstood" it, while the Siamese have "over-emphasised" it (Wijeyewardene 1985, p. 1).

Their shared but differing Buddhist religious attachments have woven an intricate relationship between the Siamese and the Chinese in Kelantan. On the one hand the Siamese need Chinese support to gain access to those areas of the economy and politics in which the Siamese are themselves quite powerless. Hence Chinese are relied upon as intermediaries and brokers by Siamese who seek employment in the wider economy and in securing a share of benefits from the larger system of ethnic and party politics. Yet the Chinese, particularly rural Chinese, need to identify with the Siamese for some pragmatic reasons too. The Chinese of Bān Klāng depend on Siamese goodwill to provide them with an identity as members of a Siamese village. Since the surrounding Malay environment may be hostile to them, it is imperative for the Chinese to underplay their "Chineseness". This they do by identifying in their social and religious behaviour with the Siamese who are more accepted by the Malays, as their long history of settlement in Kelantan, unmarked by incidents of Malay hostility, testifies.

There is also a subtle, even equivocal, relationship of power and status between the Chinese and the Siamese. While the Chinese may hold economic and political power, the Siamese clergy enjoy superior religious status in which some of the laity are included. In Bān Klāng, economic wealth does not necessarily bring about a recognition of status as such. It is the Siamese clergy and members of the religious élite who occupy the highest status positions in the village. Yet wealthy Chinese sponsor temple events regularly because this kind of religious undertaking brings them benefits in terms of increased social prestige. Even the Chinese-owned tobacco company realizes this fact; hence the donation of the costly archway. Chinese support for Siamese Buddhist temples can also be seen to result from an inability to establish a system of status of their own. In its absence the Chinese have to subscribe to that of the Siamese, hence the veneration of monks, even by town-dwelling and urban Chinese.

For generations Siamese monks and ritual experts have provided the Chinese in Kelantan with religious services, including magic and also the production of sacred artefacts, such as amulets and medallions, to a predominantly Chinese clientele. Siamese clergy are normally invited to officiate at Chinese funerals and house-blessing rites and at ceremonial activities requiring the presence of religious personalities, such as the opening of supermarkets and other business establishments. In view of this it is not surprising that medallions of famous Kelantanese monks have long been keenly sought by Chinese collectors.

The Siamese have proved to be very accommodating and tolerant towards the Chinese, even to the extent of compromising certain temple traditions. For example, adjustments are made wherever possible so that temple rites will coincide with public holidays and weekends to allow maximum participation by the Chinese, especially those from the towns. Yet despite this flexibility, the core traditions of Theravāda Buddhism, maintained and perpetuated by the Siamese, are seldom compromised. Crucial dates on Buddhist ritual calendar, such as the beginning and the end of the Lent season, and anniversaries which mark important dates during Buddha's life, such as *mākhabūchā* and *wisākhabūchā*, are celebrated on the exact days of the Buddhist calendar regardless whether they fall on weekdays. They are never "timed" to coincide with any of the Chinese holidays, not even with public and national holidays. This deep-seated core tradition of Theravāda Buddhism is in no way compromised by accommodation to the convenience of the Chinese. However, for ceremonies like *kathin*, which are not synchronized to a precise lunar calculation, adjustment of the date to coincide with public holidays is not only possible but desirable, because these are also the occasions when the temple may draw heavily upon the resources and material support of the Chinese.

Chinese and Siamese display varying levels and modalities of participation in temple events. Even though both the Siamese and the Chinese participate in the same rituals, it is during these temple functions that ethnic lines become most emphasized. In the simplest ceremonies, such as *wan phra*, ethnicity is made most explicit by the fact that the participants are almost exclusively Siamese. Likewise, during the biggest ceremonies such as the *ngān chalāung*, the expression of Siamese ethnicity also becomes most profound. Such celebrations assume a totally Siamese form and content, even when their *raison d'être* is a substantial Chinese gift, such as an archway, and even when the attendance involves a large number of Chinese.

The largest temple ceremonies also demonstrate the capacity of the Siamese to mobilize themselves on a grand scale. On any of these occasions, large numbers of the entire populations of most (if not all) Siamese villages in Kelantan and Terengganu (and also in southern Thailand) come together. By doing so they proclaim their solidarity on a scale which other ethnic groups seldom achieve. Buddhism thus becomes the main reason bringing together Siamese from various villages, not only to express their identity as an ethnic group but also their dominance in the social organization of Theravāda Buddhism. During these major functions they overwhelm the Chinese in the congregation of any particular temple.

This cycle of temple celebrations also demonstrates that Siamese Buddhism, to use Forge's term, is itself very "transportable" (1980, p. 223). Exchanges of visits and residentship between monks of temples in Kelantan and Thailand and the visit of monks to Siamese settlements without temples, together with the persistent Siamese desire to make merit even if they have to travel long distances or do so through "absentee" contributions, not only evidence the transportability of Siamese Buddhism, but they also show that it has a much wider appeal than, say, Chinese religion, which is usually confined to the village cult and seldom transcends the locality in which the cult itself originates. Such localized cults seldom attract the participation of members of other Chinese villages in the way Siamese Buddhism does.

Because it is so "transportable", Theravāda Buddhism in Kelantan remains essentially both a Siamese and a rural phenomenon. Its religious activities are confined to temples in rural villages in which the Siamese usually predominate and where a permanent community of people exists to support and staff the institution on a regular basis. Bān Klāng is perhaps an exception to this general pattern because of its substantial Chinese population, but this exception proves the rule: even in this village, the form of Buddhism that not only prevails but also flourishes remains essentially Siamese.

Pig Taboo among the Malays and Commensality Rule with the Siamese

Although commensality between the Siamese and the Malays often takes place it is not widespread and is usually limited to special occasions during which a considerable degree of restraint is observed by both parties. The general rule is that while the Siamese are expected to eat at Malay houses, the Malays are not expected to do likewise at Siamese houses. Malay avoidance of eating at Siamese houses is governed by the Islamic prohibition on certain types of food. The prohibition varies in degree from *haram* (forbidden) to *makruh* (not recommended; not encouraged). The pig heads the list of animals in the *haram* category. The prohibition is confined not only to the eating of its flesh, but also to contact with it or with any of its byproducts, whether edible or otherwise, such as lard, or for that matter any product derived from part of the animal, including leather goods made from pig skin. The dog is another *haram* animal and contact with it is equally polluting. Included in the same *haram* category is the flesh of permitted animals (such as cows, goats, and chickens) which have not been slaughtered according to Islamic prescription. However, the nature of the ritual defilement resulting from contact with such animals is not serious compared with that caused by pigs or dogs. The flesh of permitted animals but that have been killed in ways other than that prescribed by Islam cannot be consumed by Malays since it is ritually impure.

The taboo on the eating of pork or on contact with pigs and dogs has nothing to do with physical danger associated with diseases transmitted by the animals. Malay abhorrence and avoidance of these animals is attributable to a concept similar to what Mary Douglas (1966) has referred to as "ritual uncleanness". However, some Western researchers who studied Malaysian society seem to have missed the point underlying the persistent Malay avoidance of pork. Golomb, for instance, takes the stand that "even highly educated Malays may harbor beliefs about physical danger in eating well-cooked pork or foods which have come in contact with lard or pork" (1978, p. 141 and p. 211, n. 32). On the contrary, it is not physical danger that is feared most here. Irrespective of their level of education, any Malay will avoid pork or food which has come into contact with pork or lard, even if it is now common knowledge that modern pig-farming methods produce disease-free pork. In fact, the nature of taboo on pig and its derivatives is chiefly religious rather than physical; the real danger lies in the "ritual pollution" resulting from contact with it, not in the physical dangers associated with pig parasites. The remark made by Golomb fails to account for not only the religious and ritual basis of the avoidance, but also tends to be very misleading. The underlying issue is ritual defilement involving the concept of religious impurity; the real danger lies in the "ritual pollution" resulting from the contact, not in the physical dangers associated with pig parasites. The issue is ritual defilement; hence Malay phrases like *kena babi* and *bekas babi* (having been defiled by a pig, which is something of *haram* nature) come into common use. In this respect, leather shoes, wallet, gloves, handbags or any clothing accessories made from pig skin pose no physical danger to the user, but the Malays avoid using them all the same because the items are ritually unclean. Likewise, pig bristles made into brushes and other useful items are simply abhorred and avoided by Malays because of the ritual defilement they cause.

Malay avoidance of pig and the taboo on the eating of pork involves a concept which is radically different from that of the Hindu's rejection of beef-eating. Malays abhor pork because pig is an animal ritually unclean; hence all kinds of contact with it must be avoided to prevent defilement. As a contrast, the practice of not eating beef among the Hindus is attributable to their veneration of the cow as a sacred animal; contact with it is not only devoid of any defilement but is desirable, as one can see in the almost totemic status given the animal. Its dung, far from being defiling, is fully utilized by the Hindus; mixed with water it becomes a ritual cleansing agent and a kind of coating for floor surfaces; dried, it is an efficient fuel for slow-burning stoves (Harris 1975, pp. 18–19). As a contrast, pig or dog excrement is avoided at all cost by Malays, who become very concerned and uneasy if defiled by it until the source of the ritual defilement is removed.

The taboo on pork stretches beyond eating the flesh itself. The same taboo is rigidly applied to containers in which pork has been placed, which are thereby ritually polluted and should not be used by Malays unless they have undergone a special ritual cleansing. Because the nature of the defilement is religious, the removal of the impurity also involves a ritual procedure; merely washing with water and detergent is hardly adequate to remove the ritual contamination. In this procedure, called *samak*, the containers are rinsed at least seven times; six of the rinses use clean water, while one rinse, but not the last one, uses water mixed with clay or earth solution. Again, this requirement has nothing to do with the physical cleanliness of these utensils. Even if they have been washed with water and detergent, or have been sterilized to the most exacting standard, the taboo on such utensils remains unless they go through the prescribed ritual procedure.

Fear of ritual pollution is the main reason for Malays not eating at Siamese and Chinese houses, even if pork is not used in the food. The suspected source of the pollution is the serving containers or cooking utensils, which could have previously come into contact with pork or any of its products, including lard. However, many Malays quite willingly consume drinks in the same Siamese or Chinese house because it is assumed that drinking vessels are not likely to be be used to contain pork or lard. But Malays who observe strict commensality rules avoid even freshly brewed drinks, especially tea or coffee, for fear that the water could have been boiled in ritually contaminated containers. For this reason bottled or boxed drinks are often served by the Siamese to their Malay guests if the visitors are known to be very concerned about the source of the hot water. Other foods, if served, are limited to dry provisions purchased ready-made from the grocery stores, such as biscuits and pre-packed snacks, but definitely not foods prepared in the house. As for biscuits, these are served straight from the packets and seldom on a plate or dish taken directly from the kitchen. Apparently, fresh fruit does not pose any major threat of ritual defilement to Malays unless it has been sliced with ritually contaminated knives and served in equally polluted containers. Small fruits like bananas, rambutans, or mangosteens are served whole; only fruits of larger sizes, such as pineapples and watermelons, which need peeling and slicing, pose some problems when they are served to Malays.

For similar reasons Chinese food shops are avoided by Malays unless such places sell only *halal* food. Because of this, Chinese coffee shops that offer pork and other *haram* food are required by the authorities to display a prominent notice to warn unsuspecting Muslim customers. In towns like Kota Bharu, there are many shops which display these signs, but in smaller towns Chinese-owned coffee shops, which have to rely on Malay clients, serve no pork. These shops always employ Malay workers as an added assurance of the ritual purity of the food. Even then, strict Muslims avoid patronizing such shops simply because the owners are non-Muslims.

Because of the fear of ritual pollution, Malays attending temple celebrations are not expected to eat at the temple kitchen. The Malay stereotype of the Chinese and Siamese as pork-eaters who use ritually polluted cooking utensils also applies to the case of eating food prepared at the temple. However, if there is a need for a Siamese to feed his Malay neighbours or friends for one reason or another, then the host normally makes special arrangements to see that the Muslim taboo on pork is properly observed.

A wedding was held in Bān Klāng in 1982. As it is the custom for Siamese to invite Malays to their weddings and vice versa, the father of the bridegroom did so. He invited most of his Malay friends but being very conscious of the pig taboo, he chose a special day to feast them, that is, one week prior to the day of the wedding. The Malay guests were entertained and served food prepared by Malay men and women from the neighbouring villages. All the containers, cooking utensils, serving plates, and drinking vessels were borrowed from the host's Malay friends; none of his own utensils was used for the occasion. To help prepare the food, the host asked for assistance of Malay men and women, also his friends, of neighbouring villages. Cooking was done not in the host's kitchen, but instead in a small shed erected in the household's compound for this purpose. Another shed was also built to serve as the dining place. Hence, the ritual purity of both food and containers was assured.

Most of the invited Malay guests attended this special pre-wedding feast, in which *laksa* (a kind of rice noodles) was served, with the Malay guests reciprocating, as is customary, by giving the host between two and ten dollars as they were leaving. What makes this case all the more interesting is the fact that the feast for the Malays was organized one week prior to the actual wedding day, when a much bigger feast was held. On this later occasion pork was lavishly served as one of the dishes to Siamese and Chinese guests.

Since the feast for the Malays was held one week prior to the wedding day, it appears as if the groom's father was putting the Malays before his Siamese and Chinese guests. But the crucial factor which influenced the decision was nothing more than the Malay taboo on pig; had the pre-wedding feast been held immediately after the one for the Siamese, say the very next day, it could have been a social disaster in terms of inter-ethnic relationship, and obviously a clear cause of concern because the majority, if not all, of the invited Malay friends would not go to the function. No self-respecting Malay would eat at a Siamese house knowing that pigs had been slaughtered and consumed there only the day before. To Malays, the level of ritual pollution resulting from the slaughter of pigs would have been too fresh to risk contamination; the house, its compound, and most of the cooking utensils would be still freshly charged with lingering traces of pig pollution (*bekas babi*). Knowing full well that he was going to slaughter pigs at his son's wedding, the groom's father chose to entertain his Malay guests in advance to avoid any religious complications and social embarrassment.

Malays also tend to associate the culinary preferences of the Chinese and Siamese with the eating of other animals prohibited by Islam, such as the tortoise, iguana, lizard, turtle, and squirrel. The Siamese are also known to eat animals that have fallen dead due to accident, or from unexplained circumstances. According to Muslim dietary laws animals whose flesh is permissible to Muslims must first be slaughtered according to proper rites. Otherwise, the same animal, if killed by any other means, is known as *mampus* (Malay for "dead" in the sense of not being ritually slaughtered (*sembelih*), such as having been hit and killed by a speeding motor vehicle or having fallen into water and drowned, or else killed by non-Muslims). The eating of the flesh of *mampus* animals is forbidden to Muslims. Hence many cows and chickens that have died in this manner find their way into Siamese kitchens. Because of this, Siamese are considered ritually unclean by Malays.

There is, however, a concession with regard to commensality with some rural Chinese, who, because of their long residence in Malay villages, have dispensed with pork as part of their daily diet. Their eating habits have been considerably influenced by Malays to the point where some even find pork quite repulsive. These Chinese families usually exchange cooked food with their Malay neighbours as a matter of course. Tan (1982, p. 35) mentions that some rural Chinese occasionally do take pork but this is done with the utmost discretion lest Malays know about it. I suspect that this could possibly happen in isolated villages which are exclusively Chinese. Even then the Chinese take great precautions not to exhibit their purchase of pork to Malays, hiding it in innocent-looking containers whenever they have to pass through Malay villages on their way home, or when travelling on public transportation.

In the village where I grew up, there are a number of Chinese families who have been there for generations. To the best of my knowledge, pork is never part of their regular diet — at least it is not used in their kitchens. This is common knowledge among the Malay villagers. Because of the proximity of Chinese and Malay houses and because of the constant exchange of brief visits between neighbours, most housewives know exactly what takes place in one another's kitchens. Exchanges of cooked food between these Chinese families and their Malay neighbours take place regularly. Between these neighbouring families there is also constant borrowing of kitchen utensils and small food items that one runs out of now and then, such as sugar, salt, and spices. During the Chinese New Year, the Chinese give their Malay neighbours festival foods, including *kuih bakul* or *tepung bakul*, which are relished without much question being asked about their state of ritual purity. To the extent that these Chinese families have never been seen to be bringing pork into their kitchens, Malays' fear of ritual pollution from pig has been allayed.

On the whole it can be seen that the fear of ritual pollution is the reason that Malays avoid eating at Siamese or Chinese houses. Since pigs, together with dogs, are considered as animals that are ritually unclean from the Islamic point of view, and since the eating of pork and the keeping of dogs are associated with the Siamese and the Chinese, any food prepared by these two ethnic groups tends to be avoided by Malays, unless strict precautions are taken to ensure the ritual cleanliness of the cooking and serving utensils. As pigs and dogs are a source of "ritual uncleanness", contact with them or with any object which has been defiled by these two animals is abhorred by Malays. It is the ritual aspect of the defilement rather than the physical danger associated with pork-eating and contact with dogs that has become the decisive factor in setting the rules governing commensality and exchange of foods between Malays and their non-Muslim neighbours.

REFERENCES

Abdullah bin Abdul Kadir, Munshi. *Kesah pelayaran Abdullah*. Singapore: Malaya Publishing House, 1960.

Asmah Hj. Omar. "Patterns of Language Communication in Malaysia". *Southeast Asian Journal of Social Science* 13, no. 1 (1985): 19–28.

Baker, J.A. "Notes on the Meaning of Some Malay Words, Part III (Kedah words)". *Journal of the Malayan Branch of the Royal Asiatic Society* 17, pt. 1 (1939): 107–20.

Banks, David J. "Pluralism East and West, Some Parallels and Differences: Malaysia and the Caribbean". *Contributions to Asian Studies* 7 (1975): 17–31.

―――. "Politics and Ethnicity on the Thai-Malay Frontier: The Historical Role of the Thai-Speaking Muslims of Kedah". *Kabar Seberang* 7 (1980): 98–113.

Barth, Fredrik, ed. *Ethnic Groups and Boundaries: The Social Organisation of Culture Difference*. London: George Allen and Unwin, 1969.

Benjamin, Geoffrey. "Indigenous Religious Systems of the Peninsular Malaysia". In *The Imagination of Reality: Essay in Southeast Asian Coherence Systems*, edited by A. Yengoyan and A.L. Becker. Norwood, NJ: Ablex, 1979.

Bonney, R. *Kedah 1771–1821: The Search for Security and Independence*. Kuala Lumpur: Oxford University Press, 1971.

Brown, C.C. *Studies in Country Malay*. London: Luzac, 1956.

Bunnag, Jane. *Buddhist Monk, Buddhist Layman: A Study of Urban Monastic Organization in Thailand*. Cambridge Studies in Social Anthropology no. 6. Cambridge: Cambridge University Press, 1973.

Burr, Angela. "Religious Institutional Diversity — Social Structural and Conceptual Unity: Islam and Buddhism in a Southern Thai Coastal Fishing Village". *Journal of the Siam Society* 60 (1972): 183–215.

Carstens, Sharon A. "Pulai: Memories of a Gold Mining Settlement in Ulu Kelantan". *Journal of the Malaysian Branch of the Royal Asiatic Society* 53, pt. 1 (1980): 50–67.

Chan Su Ming. "Kelantan and Trengganu, 1909–1939". *Journal of the Malaysian Branch of the Royal Asiatic Society* 38, pt. 1 (1965): 159–98.

Chia Ai Yet. "Pemujaan Dewa Penjaga: Satu Kajian Kes di Kampung Kasar, Pasir Mas, Kelantan". BA dissertation, Universiti Kebangsaan Malaysia, Bangi, 1981.

Clammer, John R. "Overseas Chinese Assimilation and Resinification: A Malaysian Case Study". *Southeast Asian Journal of Social Science* 3, no. 2 (1975): 9–23.

_____ . *The Ambiguity of Identity: Ethnicity Maintenance and Change among the Straits Chinese Community of Malaysia and Singapore.* Occasional Paper no. 54. Singapore: Institute of Southeast Asian Studies, 1979.

Cook, Nerida M. "The Position of Nuns in Thai Buddhism: The Parameters of Religious Recognition". MA thesis, Australian National University, 1981.

Cuisinier, Jeanne. *Danses magiques de Kelantan.* Paris: Institut d'Ethnologie, 1936.

Cushman, J.W. and A.C. Milner. "Eighteenth and Nineteenth-Century Chinese Accounts of the Malay Peninsula". *Journal of the Malaysian Branch of the Royal Asiatic Society* 52, pt. 1 (1979): 1–56.

Davies, I. Talog. "'Malay' as Defined in the States Malay Reservation Enactments". *Intisari* 1, no. 2 (n.d.): 26–28.

Davis, Richard B. *Muang Metaphysics: A Study of Northern Thai Myth and Ritual.* Studies in Thai Anthropology 1. Bangkok: Pandora, 1984.

De Vos, George. "Ethnic Pluralism: Conflict and Accommodation". In *Ethnic Identity: Cultural Continuities and Change,* edited by George De Vos and Lola Romanucci-Ross. Palo Alto: Mayfield Publishing, 1975.

De Young, John E. *Village Life in Modern Thailand.* Berkeley: University of California Press, 1966.

DeBernardi, Jean. "The Hungry Ghosts Festival: A Convergence of Religion and Politics in the Chinese Community of Penang, Malaysia". *Southeast Asian Journal of Social Science* 12, no. 1 (1984): 25–34.

Douglas, Mary. *Purity and Danger: An Analysis of Concepts of Pollution and Taboo.* Harmondsworth: Penguin, 1966.

Downs, Richard. "A Kelantan Village of Malaya". In *Contemporary Change in Traditional Societies,* vol. III, edited by Julian H. Steward. Chicago: University of Illinois Press, 1967.

Farrer, R.J. "A Buddhist Purification Ceremony". *Journal of the Malayan Branch of the Royal Asiatic Society* 11, pt. 2 (1933): 261–63.

Firth, Raymond. *Malay Fishermen.* 2nd ed. London: Routledge and Kegan Paul, 1966 (1st ed., 1946).

Forge, A. "Balinese Religion and Indonesian Identity". In *Indonesia: The Making of a Culture,* edited by J.J. Fox. Canberra: Research School of Pacific Studies, Australian National University, 1980.

Freedman, Maurice. "The Growth of a Plural Society in Malaya". *Pacific Affairs* 33, no. 2 (1960): 158–68.

Funston, N. John. "The Origin of Parti Islam Se Malaysia". *Journal of Southeast Asian Studies* 7, no. 1 (1976): 58–73.

————. *Malay Politics in Malaysia: A Study of the United Malays Nationalist Organisation and Party Islam.* Kuala Lumpur: Heinemann, 1980.

Geertz, Clifford. *The Interpretation of Cultures.* New York: Basic Books, 1973.

Ghulam-Sarwar Yousof. "*Nora Chatri* in Kedah: A Preliminary Report". *Journal of the Malaysian Branch of the Royal Asiatic Society* 55, pt. 1 (1982): 53–61.

————. "Feasting of the Spirits: The *Berjamu* Ritual Performance in the Kelantanese *Wayang Siam* Shadow Play". *Kajian Malaysia* 1, no. 1 (1983): 95–115.

Gimlette, J.D. "A Curious Kelantan Charm". *Journal of the Straits Branch of the Royal Asiatic Society* 82 (1920): 116–18.

Ginsburg, Henry D. "The Manora Dance Drama: An Introduction". *Journal of the Siam Society* 60 (1972): 169–81.

Golomb, Louis. *Brokers of Morality: Thai Ethnic Adaptation in a Rural Malaysian Setting.* Hawaii: University of Hawaii Press, 1978.

Government of Malaysia. *1980 Population and Housing Census of Malaysia:*

State Population Report, Kelantan. Kuala Lumpur: Department of Statistics, 1983.

Gullick, J.M. *Malaya.* London: Ernest Benn, 1963.

Haas, Mary R. *Thai-English Student's Dictionary.* Stanford, CA: Stanford University Press, 1964.

Harris, Marvin. *Cows, Pigs, Wars and Witches: The Riddle of Culture.* London: Hutchinson, 1975.

Hirschman, Charles. "Ethnic Stratification in West Malaysia". Ph.D. dissertation, University of Wisconsin, 1972.

Ishii, Yoneo. *Sangha, State, and Society: Thai Buddhism in History.* Kyoto: Center for Southeast Asian Studies, Kyoto University, 1986.

Ismail Bakti. "*Bunga mas* — Golden Flowers: Gift or Tribute". *Malaysia in History* (Special issue) 22 (1979): 153–55.

Ismail, Mohamed Yusoff. "The Siamese Village of Aril: A Study of an Ethnic Minority Settlement". MA thesis, Monash University, 1977.

_____. *The Siamese of Aril: A Study of an Ethnic Minority Village.* Monograph no. 3, Faculty of Social Sciences and the Humanities. Bangi: Universiti Kebangsaan Malaysia, 1980*a*.

_____. "The Social History of a Siamese Village in Kelantan". Paper presented at the 8th International Association of Historians of Asia, 1980*b*, Kuala Lumpur.

_____. "Tradition and Change in Aril, a Siamese Village in Kelantan". *Mankind* 13, no. 3 (1982): 252–63.

_____. "Buddhism and Ethnicity: The Case of the Siamese of Kelantan". *SOJOURN: Social Issues in Southeast Asia* 2, no. 2 (1987): 231–54.

_____. "Kata-kata Pinjaman Thai dalam Dialek Kelantan" [Thai loanwords in Kelantanese dialect]. *Warisan Kelantan* 8 (1989): 42–50.

_____. "Buddhism among the Siamese of Kelantan: Minority Religion in a Muslim State". *Jurnal Antropologi dan Sosiologi* 18 (1990*a*): 55–69.

_____. "Siamese Buddhism in a Malay State: Some Notes on Temple Organisation in Kelantan, Malaysia". In *Radical Conservatism: Buddhism in the Contemporary World: Articles in Honour of Bhikkhu Buddhadasa's 84th Birthday Anniversary,* edited by Sulak Sivaraksa et al. Bangkok: Sathirakoses-Nagapradipa Foundation, 1990*b*.

————. "Membuat Pahala Sebagai Ritus Kebiaraan di Kalangan Penganut Agama Buddha di Kelantan" [Merit-making as a monastic rite among the Buddhists of Kelantan]. *Sarjana* 6 (1990*c*): 51–67.

Johnston, David B. "Bandit, *Nakleng*, and Peasant in Rural Thai Society". *Contributions to Asian Studies* 15 (1980): 90–101.

Kassim Ahmad, ed. *Kisah Pelayaran Abdullah*. Kuala Lumpur: Oxford University Press, 1960.

Kaufman, Howard Keva. *Bangkhuad: A Community Study of Thailand*. Monograph for the Association of Asian Studies no. 10. Locust Valley, NY: J.J. Augustin, 1960.

Kershaw, Roger. "The Thais of Kelantan: A Socio-Political Study of an Ethnic Outpost". Ph.D. thesis, University of London, 1969.

————. "The Chinese in Kelantan, West Malaysia, as Mediators of Political Integration to the Kelantan Thais". *Review of Southeast Asian Studies* 3, nos. 3 and 4 (1973): 1–10.

————. "Menace and Reassurance in Malay Circumcision: A Note on Some Attitudes of Kelantan Malays". *Journal of the Siam Society* 67 (1979): 116–22.

————. "Frontiers within Frontiers: The Persistence of Thai Ethnicity in Kelantan, Malaysia" (Review article). *Journal of the Siam Society* 68 (1980): 145–58.

————. "Towards a Theory of Peranakan Chinese Identity in an Outpost of Thai Buddhism". *Journal of the Siam Society* 69 (1981): 74–106.

————. "A Little Drama of Ethnicity: Some Sociological Aspects of the Kelantan Manora". *Southeast Asian Journal of Social Science* 10 (1982): 69–95.

————. "Native but Not Bumiputra: Crisis and Complexity in the Political Status of the Kelantan Thais after Independence". *Contributions to Southeast Asian Ethnography* 3 (1984): 46–71.

Kessler, Clive S. "Islam, Society and Political Behaviour: Some Comparative Implications of the Malay Case". *British Journal of Sociology* 23 (1972): 33–50.

————. "Muslim Identity and Political Behaviour in Kelantan". In *Kelantan: Religion, Society and Politics in a Malay State*, edited by William R. Roff. Kuala Lumpur: Oxford University Press, 1974.

_____. *Islam and Politics in a Malay State: Kelantan 1838–1969.* Ithaca and London: Cornell University Press, 1978.

Keyes, Charles F. *The Golden Peninsula: Culture and Adaptation in Mainland Southeast Asia.* New York: Macmillan, 1977.

_____. "Mother or Mistress but Never a Monk: Buddhist Notions of Female Gender in Rural Thailand". *American Ethnologist* 11 (1984): 223–41.

Khantipalo, Bhikkhu. *Buddhism Explained: An Introduction to the Teachings of the Lord Buddha.* 3rd ed. Bangkok: Thai Watana Panich Press, 1970.

Khasnor Johan. "The *Bunga Emas* in Malay-Siamese Relations". *Journal of the Historical Society, University Malaya* 4 (1965/66): 11–16.

Khoo Kay Kim. "Islam and Politics in a Malay State: Kelantan 1838–1969" (Review article). *Journal of Southeast Asian Studies* 11 (1980): 187–94.

King, Victor T. "Ethnicity in Borneo: An Anthropological Problem". *Southeast Asian Journal of Social Science* 10 (1982): 23–43.

Klausner, William J. "Popular Buddhism in Northeast Thailand". In *Cross-Cultural Understanding: Epistemology in Anthropology,* edited by F.S.C. Northrop and Helen H. Livingston. New York: Harper and Row, 1964.

Klinkert, H.C., ed. *Verhaal van de reis van Abdoellah naar Kalantan en van zijne reis naar Djeddah, in het Malaeich.* Leiden: E.J. Brill, 1889.

Lester, Robert C. *Theravada Buddhism in Southeast Asia.* Ann Arbor: University of Michigan Press, 1973.

Levenberg, Blanche. "The Monk's Bowl". *Visakha Puja,* 2515 [1972], pp. 90–94.

Maeda, Kiyoshige. *Alor Janggus: A Chinese Community in Malaya.* Kyoto: Center for Southeast Asian Studies, Kyoto University, 1967.

Marriott, H. "A Fragment of the History of Trengganu and Kelantan". *Journal of the Straits Branch of the Royal Asiatic Society* 72 (1916): 3–23.

Middlebrook, S.M. "Pulai: An Early Chinese Settlement in Kelantan". *Journal of the Malayan Branch of the Royal Asiatic Society* 11 (1933): 151–56.

Mills, L.A. "British Malaya: 1824–1867". *Journal of the Malayan Branch of the Royal Asiatic Society* 1 (1925): 1–338.

Moerman, Michael. *Agricultural Change and Peasant Choice in a Thai Village.*

Berkeley: University of California Press, 1968.

Mohamed b. Nik Mohd. Salleh. "Kelantan in Transition: 1891–1910". In *Kelantan: Religion, Society and Politics in a Malay State*, edited by William R. Roff. Kuala Lumpur: Oxford University Press, 1974.

Mohammad bin Haji Idris. "Penghijrahan Orang-Orang China ke Kelantan" [Chinese migration to Kelantan]. *Jebat* (Jabatan Sejarah, Universiti Kebangsaan Malaysia) 5, no. 6 (1975): 82–95.

Mokhzani, B.A.R. "Credit in a Malay Peasant Economy". Ph.D. dissertation, University of London, 1973.

Muhammad Salleh b. Wan Musa with S. Othman Kelantan. "Theological Debates: Wan Musa b. Haji Abdul Samad and His Family". In *Kelantan: Religion, Society and Politics in a Malay State*, edited by William R. Roff. Kuala Lumpur: Oxford University Press, 1974.

Nagata, Judith A. "What Is a Malay? Situational Selection of Ethnic Identity in a Plural Society". *American Ethnologist* 1 (1974): 331–50.

Nanamoli Thera, trans. *The Pāṭimokkha: 227 Fundamental Rules of a Bhikkhu*. Bangkok: Social Science Association Press, 1966.

Narada, Maha Thera. *The Buddha and His Teachings*. Colombo: n.p., 1973.

Nash, Manning. *Peasant Citizens: Politics, Religion, and Modernisation in Kelantan, Malaysia*. Papers in International Studies, Southeast Asia Series no. 31. Athens, OH: Center for International Studies, Southeast Asia Program, Ohio University, 1974.

Nash, Manning et al. *Anthropological Studies in Theravada Buddhism*. Cultural Report Series no. 13, Southeast Asia. New Haven: Yale University, 1966.

Nicolas, Rene. "Le Lakhon Nora ou Lakhon Chatri et les origines du théâtre classique siamois". *Journal of the Siam Society* 18 (1924): 84–110.

O'Connor, Richard Allan. "Urbanism and Religion: Community, Hierarchy and Sanctity in Urban Thai Temples". Ph.D. dissertation, Cornell University, 1978.

Pasir Puteh District Office File no. 405/28. Arkib Negara Malaysia, 19 November 1928.

Pepys, W.E. "A Kelantan Glossary". *Journal of the Straits Branch of the Royal Asiatic Society* 74 (1916): 303–21.

Phillips, Herbert P. *Thai Peasant Personality: The Patterning of Interpersonal Behaviour in the Village of Bang Chan*. Berkeley: University of California Press, 1965.

Pillsbury, Barbara L.K. "Pig and Policy: Maintenance of Boundaries between Han and Muslim Chinese". *Ethnic Groups* 1 (1976): 151–62.

Purcell, Victor. *The Chinese in Malaya*. London: Oxford University Press, 1948.

Rahmat Saripan. *Perkembangan Politik Melayu Kelantan 1776–1842* [The development of Kelantanese Malay politics, 1776–1842]. Kuala Lumpur: Dewan Bahasa dan Pustaka, 1979.

Rahula, Walpola. *History of Buddhism in Ceylon: The Anurādhapura Period 3rd Century BC–10th Century AC*. 2nd ed. Colombo: M.D. Gunasena, 1966 (1st ed., 1956).

_____ . *What the Buddha Taught*. 2nd ed. Bedford: Gordon Fraser, 1967 (1st ed., 1959).

Raja Mohar bin Raja Badiozaman. "Malay Land Reservation and Alienation". *Intisari* 1 (n.d.): 19–25.

Raybeck, Douglas. "Ethnicity and Accommodation: Malay-Chinese Relations in Kelantan, Malaysia". *Ethnic Groups* 2 (1980): 241–68.

Rentse, Anker. "History of Kelantan I". *Journal of the Malayan Branch of the Royal Asiatic Society* 12 (1934): 44–62.

Reynolds, Craig J. "Buddhist Cosmography in Thai History, with Special Reference to Nineteenth-Century Culture Change". *Journal of Asian Studies* 35 (1976): 203–20.

Ridley, Henry N. *The Flora of the Malay Peninsula*. Vol. I. London: Reeve, 1922*a*.

_____ . *The Flora of the Malay Peninsula*. Vol. V. London: Reev, 1922*b*.

Roff, William R., ed. *Kelantan: Religion, Society and Politics in a Malay State*. Kuala Lumpur: Oxford University Press, 1974.

Sadka, Emily. *The Protected Malay States 1874–1895*. Kuala Lumpur: University of Malaya Press, 1968.

Schumann, Hans Wolfgang. *Buddhism*. London: Rider, 1973.

Sharom Ahmat. "Kedah-Siam Relations, 1821–1905". *Journal of the Siam Society* 59 (1971): 97–117.

Sheppard, Mubin. "Manora: The Ballet of Ligor". *Straits Times Annual*, 1959, pp. 12–15.

_____ . "Manora in Kelantan". *Journal of the Malaysian Branch of the Royal*

Asiatic Society 46 (1973): 161–70.

Skeat, W.W. "Reminiscences of the Cambridge University Expedition to the North-Eastern Malay States, 1899–1900". *Journal of the Malayan Branch of the Royal Asiatic Society* 26 (1953): 9–147.

Skinner, C. *The Civil War in Kelantan in 1839*. Monograph no. 2. Kuala Lumpur: Malaysian Branch of the Royal Asiatic Society, 1965.

Smith, Michael G. *The Plural Society in the British West Indies*. Berkeley: University of California Press, 1965.

_____ . "Institutional and Political Conditions of Pluralism". In *Pluralism in Africa*, edited by L. Kuper and M.G. Smith. Berkeley: University of California Press, 1971.

So Sethaputra. *New Model Thai-English Dictionary*. Phra Nakhon: Thai Wathanaapaanit, 1971 [2514 B.E.].

Steffen, A. "Clay Tablets from Caves in Siamese Malaya (With Notes by N. Annandale)". *Man* 2, no. 125 (1902): 177–80.

Strauch, Judith. "Multiple Ethnicities in Malaysia: The Shifting Relevance of Alternative Chinese Categories". *Modern Asian Studies* 15 (1984): 235–60.

Sturrock, A.J. "Some Notes on the Kelantan Dialect, and Some Comparisons with the Dialects of Perak and Central Pahang". *Journal of the Straits Branch of the Royal Asiatic Society* 62 (1912): 1–7.

Suchiip Punyaanuphaap. *Potchanaanukrom sap phraputthasatsaanaa thaj-angkrit lae angkrit-thaj* [Dictionary of Buddhist terms: Thai–English and English–Thai]. 2nd ed. Phra Nakhon: Kasem Bannakich, 1971 [2514 B.E.].

Surin Pitsuwan. *Islam and Malay Nationalism: A Case Study of the Malay-Muslims of Southern Thailand*. Ph.D. dissertation, Harvard University, 1982.

Swearer, Donald K. *Wat Haripunjaya: A Study of the Royal Temple of the Buddha's Relic, Lamphun, Thailand*. Missoula, MT: Scholars Press, 1976a.

_____ . "The Role of Layman *Extraordinaire* in Northern Thai Buddhism". *Journal of the Siam Society* 64 (1976b): 149–68.

Swift, M.G. *Malay Peasant Society in Jelebu*. London School of Economics Monograph on Social Anthropology no. 2. London: Athlone Press, 1965.

Taib, Abdullah and Mohamed Yusoff Ismail. "The Social Structure". In *The Political Economy of Malaysia*, edited by E.K. Fisk and H. Osman-Rani. Kuala Lumpur: Oxford University Press, 1982.

Tambiah, Stanley Jeyaraja. *Buddhism and Spirit Cults in Northeast Thailand*. Cambridge: Cambridge University Press, 1970.

_____ . *World Conqueror and World Renouncer: A Study of Buddhism and Polity in Thailand against a Historical Background*. Cambridge: Cambridge University Press, 1976.

_____ . *Buddhist Saints of the Forest and the Cult of the Amulets*. Cambridge: Cambridge University Press, 1984.

Tan Chee Beng. "Baba Chinese, Non-Baba Chinese and Malays: A Note on Ethnic Interaction in Malacca". *Southeast Asian Journal of Social Science* 7 (1979): 20–29.

_____ . "Peranakan Chinese in Northeast Kelantan with Special Reference to Chinese Religion". *Journal of the Malaysian Branch of the Royal Asiatic Society* 55 (1982): 26–52.

_____ . "Chinese Religion in Malaysia: A General View". *Asian Folklore Studies* 42 (1983): 217–52.

Teeuw, A. and D.K. Wyatt, eds. *Hikayat Patani*. The Hague: Martinus Nijhoff, 1970.

Tennant, Paul. "Pluralism in West Malaysian Politics". *Contributions to Asian Studies* 7 (1975): 79–86.

Teo Hui Bek. *The Flue-Cured Virginia Tobacco Industry in Malaysia*. Kota Bharu, Kelantan: National Tobacco Board, Malaysia, 1979.

Terwiel, B.J. "The Five Precepts and Ritual in Rural Thailand". *Journal of the Siam Society* 60 (1972): 333–43.

_____ . *Monks and Magic: An Analysis of Religious Ceremonies in Central Thailand*. 2nd rev. ed. Scandinavian Institute of Asian Studies Monograph Series no. 24. London and Malmö: Curzon Press, 1979 (1st ed., 1975).

Textor, Robert Bayard. "An Inventory of Non-Buddhist Supernatural Objects in a Central Thai Village". Ph.D. dissertation, Cornell University, 1960.

Tobias, Stephen F. "Buddhism, Belonging and Detachment — Some Paradoxes of Chinese Ethnicity in Thailand". *Journal of Asian Studies* 36

(1977): 303–25.

Tweedie, Michael W.F. "An Early Chinese Account of Kelantan". *Journal of Malayan Branch of the Royal Asiatic Society* 26 (1963): 216–19.

Vella, Walter F. *Siam under Rama III 1824–1851*. Monograph for the Association for Asian Studies. New York: J.J. Augustin, 1957.

Wang Gungwu. "An Early Chinese Visitor to Kelantan". *Malaya in History* 6 (1960): 31–35.

————. *The Chinese Minority in Southeast Asia*. Southeast Asia Research Paper Series no. 1. Singapore: Chopmen Enterprises, 1978.

Wee, Vivienne. " 'Buddhism' in Singapore". In *Singapore: Society in Transition*, edited by Riaz Hassan. Kuala Lumpur: Oxford University Press, 1976.

Wells, Kenneth E. *Thai Buddhism, Its Rites and Activities*. Bangkok: Suriyabun Publishers, 1975 (1st ed., 1939).

Wijeyewardene, Gehan. "Some Aspects of Rural Life in Thailand". In *Thailand: Social and Economic Studies in Development*, edited by T.H. Silcock. Canberra: Australian National University Press, 1967.

————. "The Theravada Compact and the Karen". Paper presented at the Department of Anthropology, Research School of Pacific Studies, Australian National University, 11 September 1985.

Winzeler, Robert L. "Ethnic Complexity and Ethnic Relationship in an East Coast Malay Town". *Southeast Asian Journal of Social Science* 2 (1974): 45–61.

————. "The Rural Chinese of the Kelantan Plain". *Journal of the Malaysian Branch of the Royal Asiatic Society* 54 (1981): 1–23.

————. *Ethnic Relations in Kelantan: A Study of the Chinese and Thai as Ethnic Minorities in a Malay State*. Singapore: Oxford University Press, 1985.

Wyatt, David K. "Nineteenth Century Kelantan: A Thai View". In *Kelantan: Religion, Society and Politics in a Malay State*, edited by William R. Roff. Kuala Lumpur: Oxford University Press, 1974.

THE AUTHOR

Mohamed Yusoff Ismail is an Associate Professor in the Department of Anthropology and Sociology, Universiti Kebangsaan Malaysia. His research interests include anthropology of religion, Theravāda Buddhism in Southeast Asia, ethnicity and minority studies. In June 1992 he was seconded to the Faculty of Development Science, UKM Sabah Campus, as Deputy Dean.